CW00455606

Profanations

Translated by Jeff Fort

Profanations

Giorgio Agamben

ZONE BOOKS · NEW YORK

2007

ZONE BOOKS
1226 Prospect Avenue
Brooklyn, NY 11218

Second Printing 2010

Originally published as *Profanazioni* © 2005 Nottetempo.

Printed in the United States of America.

Distributed by The MIT Press,
Cambridge, Massachusetts, and London, England

Library of Congress Cataloging-in-Publication Data

Agamben, Giorgio, 1942–
    [Profanazioni English]
    Profanations / Giorgio Agamben ; translated by Jeff Fort.
    p. cm.
Includes bibliographical references.
ISBN 978-1-890951-82-5
1. Aesthetics. 2. Art — Philosophy. I. Title.
BH39.A3213 2007
111'.85–dc22

                                                        2007023901

Contents

Translator's Note

I would like to thank Kevin Attell for contributing his translation, "In Praise of Profanation," which he prepared at Agamben's request for an oral presentation of this text in English in January 2005. I would also like to thank Tommaso Giartosio for his helpful suggestions.

Chapter One

Genius

> Now my charms are all o'erthrown
> And what strength I have's mine own.
> — Prospero to the audience in *The Tempest*

In Latin, *Genius* was the name used for the god who becomes each man's guardian at the moment of birth. The etymology is transparent and remains visible linguistically in the very proximity appearing between genius and generation. That Genius is related to generation is evident in any case due to the fact that in Latin, the "genial" object par excellence was the bed, the *lectus genialis*, because it is in bed that the act of generation is accomplished. Birthdays are sacred to Genius, and for that reason we still use the adjective *genetliaco* (birthday) in Italian. Despite the odious, now-inevitable Anglo-Saxon refrain, the presents and parties with which we celebrate birthdays are a memory of the feast and sacrifices offered to Genius by Roman families on birthdays. Horace speaks of pure wine, of a two-month-old piglet, of an "immolated" lamb, meaning one that is sprinkled with sauce for the sacrifice. It seems, though, that originally there was only incense, wine, and delicious honey cake, because Genius, the god who presides over birth, did not like blood sacrifices.

9

"He is called my Genius, because he generated me (*Genius meus nominatur, quia me genuit*)." But that is not all. Genius was not only the personification of sexual energy. Certainly, every man had his Genius and every woman her Juno, both of which manifested the fertility that generates and perpetuates life. But as the term *ingenium* — that is, the sum of physical and moral qualities innate in the one who is born — indicates, Genius was, in a certain way, the divinization of the person, the principle that governed and expressed his entire existence. For this reason, it was not the pubis but the forehead that was associated with Genius; the gesture of bringing the hand to the forehead — which we enact almost without realizing it in moments of confusion and disorientation, when we seem almost to have forgotten ourselves — recalls the ritual gesture of the cult of Genius (*unde venerantes deum tangimus frontem*).[1] And since this god is, in a sense, what is most intimate and most our own, he must be placated and his favor maintained in every aspect and at every moment of life.

A Latin phrase perfectly expresses the secret relationship each person must maintain with his own Genius: *indulgere genio*. One must consent to Genius and abandon oneself to him; one must grant him everything he asks for, for his exigencies are our exigencies, his happiness our happiness. Even if his — our! — requirements seem unreasonable and capricious, it is best to accept them without argument. If in order to write you need — he needs! — a certain light yellow paper, a certain special pen, a certain dim light shining from the left, it is useless to tell yourself that just any pen will do, that any paper and any light will suffice. If life is not worth living without that light blue linen shirt (for goodness' sake, not the white one with the collar of an office worker!), if without those long cigarettes with black paper you just don't see any reason to go on, then there's no point in repeating to yourself that these are no more than little manias, that now is the time to be over and done with them. In Latin, *Genium suum defraudare*, to defraud one's own genius, means to make one's life miserable, to cheat oneself, in Latin. But the life that turns away from death and responds without hesitation to the impetus of the genius that engendered it is called *genialis*, genial.

But this most intimate and personal god is also that which is most impersonal in us; it is the personalization of what, in us, goes beyond and exceeds us. "Genius is our life not insofar as it was originated by us, but rather insofar as we originate from it." If it seems to be identified with us, it is only in order to reveal itself immediately afterward as more than us, and to show us that we are more and less than ourselves. Comprehending the conception of man implicit in Genius means understanding that man is not only an ego and an individual consciousness, but rather that from birth to death he is accompanied by an impersonal, preindividual element. Man is thus a single being with two phases; he is a being that results from the complex dialectic between a part that has yet to be individuated and lived and another part that is marked by fate and individual experience. But the impersonal, nonindividual part is not a past we have left behind once and for all and that we may eventually recall in memory; it is still present in us, still with us, near to us and inseparable from us, for both good and ill. Genius' youthful face and long, fluttering wings signify that he does not know time, that we feel him quivering as closely within us as he did when we were children, breathing and beating in our feverish temples like an immemorial present. That is why a birthday cannot be the commemoration of a past day but, like every true celebration, must be an abolition of time — the epiphany and presence of Genius. This inescapable presence prevents us from enclosing ourselves within a substantial identity and shatters the ego's pretension to be sufficient unto itself.

It has been said that spirituality is above all an awareness that the individuated being is not completely individuated but still contains a certain nonindividuated share of reality, which must be not only preserved but also respected and, in a way, even honored, as one honors one's debts. But Genius is not merely spirituality and is not just concerned with the things that we customarily regard as higher and more noble. Everything in us that is impersonal is genial. The force that pushes the blood through our veins or that plunges us into sleep, the unknown power in our body that gently regulates and distributes its warmth or that relaxes or contracts the fibers of our muscles — that too is genial. It is Genius that we obscurely sense in the intimacy of our physiological life, in which what is most one's own is also strange and impersonal, and in which what is nearest somehow remains distant and escapes mastery. If we did not abandon ourselves to Genius, if we were only ego and consciousness, we would not even be able to urinate. Living with Genius means, in this sense, living in the intimacy of a strange being, remaining constantly in relation to a zone of nonconsciousness. But this zone of nonconsciousness is not repression; it does not shift or displace an experience from consciousness to the unconscious, where this experience would be sedimented as a troubling past, waiting to resurface in symptoms and neuroses. This intimacy with a zone of nonconsciousness is

12

an everyday mystical practice, in which the ego, in a sort of special, joyous esoterism, looks on with a smile at its own undoing and, whether it's a matter of digesting food or illuminating the mind, testifies incredulously to its own incessant dissolution and disappearance. *Genius* is our life insofar as it does not belong to us.

We must therefore consider the subject as a force field of tensions whose antithetical poles are Genius and Ego. This field is traversed by two conjoined but opposed forces: one that moves from the individual to the impersonal and another that moves from the impersonal to the individual. The two forces coexist, intersect, separate, but can neither emancipate themselves completely from each other nor identify with each other perfectly. What, then, is the best way for Ego to testify to Genius? Suppose the ego wants to write — not to write this or that work, but simply to write, period. This desire means: I (Ego) feel that somewhere Genius exists, that there is in me an impersonal power that presses toward writing. But this Genius, who has never taken up a pen (much less a computer) — has no inclination to produce a work. One writes in order to become impersonal, to become genial, and yet, in writing, we individuate ourselves as authors of this or that work; we move away from Genius, who can never have the form of an ego, much less that of an author. Every attempt by Ego, by the personal element, to appropriate Genius, to force him to sign in one's own name, is necessarily destined to fail. Hence we have the pertinence and success of ironic operations like those of the avant-garde, in which the presence of Genius is attested to in the decreation and destruction of the work. But if the only work worthy of Genius is the one been revoked and undone, and if the truly genial artist is the artist without a work, then the Duchamp-Ego will never be able to coincide with Genius and, to the admiration of all, will pass through the world like the melancholic proof of its own nonexistence, like the ill-famed bearer of its own unworking.

That is why the encounter with Genius is terrible. The life that maintains the tension between the personal and the impersonal, between Ego and Genius, is called poetic. But the feeling that occurs when Genius exceeds us on every side is called panic — panic at something that comes over us and is infinitely greater than what we believe ourselves able to bear. For this reason, most people flee in terror before the part of themselves that is impersonal, or else they seek hypocritically to reduce it to their own miniscule stature. What is rejected as impersonal, then, can reappear in the form of symptoms and tics that are even more impersonal, or grimaces that are even more excessive. But more laughable and fatuous than this is someone who experiences the encounter with Genius as a privilege, the Poet who strikes a pose and puts on airs or, worse, feigns humility and gives thanks for the grace received. In the face of Genius, no one is great; we are all equally small. But some let themselves be shaken and traversed by Genius to the point of falling apart. Others, more serious but less happy, refuse to impersonate the impersonal, to lend their lips to a voice that does not belong to them.

The rank of every being can be defined by an ethics of relationships with Genius. The lowest rank comprises those — and sometimes they are very famous authors — who think of their genius as a sort of personal sorcerer ("Everything turns out so well for me!" — "If only you, my Genius, do not abandon me..."). How much more amiable and sober is the poet who does without this sordid accomplice, because he knows that "the absence of God helps."[2]

Children take a particular pleasure in hiding, not because they will be found in the end, but by the very act of hiding, of being concealed in a laundry basket or a cabinet, of curling up in the corner of an attic to the point of almost disappearing. There is an incomparable joy, a special excitement that children are unwilling to renounce for any reason. This childlike excitement is the source of both Robert Walser's voluptuous pleasure in securing the conditions of his illegibility (the micrograms) and Walter Benjamin's stubborn desire to go unrecognized. This pleasure and this desire are the guardians of the solitary *glory* revealed to children in their secret lairs. For the poet celebrates his triumph in nonrecognition, just like the child discovers the *genius loci* of his hiding place with trepidation.

According to Gilbert Simondon, emotion is the way we relate to the preindividual. To have emotion, to be moved, is to feel the impersonal within us, to experience Genius as anguish or joy, safety or fear.

On the threshold of the zone of nonconsciousness, Ego must shed its own properties; it must be moved. Passion is the tightrope, stretched between us and Genius, on which our funambulant life steps forward. Even before we wonder at the world outside us, what awes and stuns us is the presence within us of a part that is forever immature, infinitely adolescent, and hesitant to cross the threshold of any individuation. It is this elusive young boy, this *puer*, who stubbornly pushes us toward others, in whom we seek precisely the emotion that remains incomprehensible in ourselves, hoping that by some miracle it

15

will be clarified and elucidated in the mirror of the other. Witnessing the pleasure and the passion of others is the supreme emotion and the first politics because we seek in the other the relationship with Genius which we are incapable of grasping on our own; our secret delight and our proud and lofty agony.

In time, Genius took on a twofold aspect and an ethical coloration. The sources — influenced, perhaps, by the Greek theme of the two daimons within each man — speak of a good genius and a bad genius, of a white (*albus*) genius and a black (*ater*) one. The first pushes and coaxes us toward good; the second corrupts us and inclines us toward evil. Horace is no doubt right to suggest that there is, in reality, one Genius who changes — by turns candid and shadowy, sometimes wise and sometimes depraved. In other words, what changes is not Genius but our relationship to him, turning from luminous and clear to shadowy and opaque. Our own vital principle, the companion who orients our existence and renders it amiable, is then suddenly transformed into a kind of silent, hidden outlaw who follows our every move like a shadow and secretly conspires against us. Roman art thus represents two *genii* side by side: one who carries a burning torch and another, a harbinger of death, who overturns it.

In this belated moralization, the paradox of Genius fully emerges: if Genius is *our* life, insofar as it does *not* belong to us, then we must answer for something for which we are not responsible. The childlike face of our own salvation and of our own ruin both is and is not our face.

The analogue of Genius in the Christian tradition is the guardian angel — or, more precisely, two angels. One is good and holy, guiding us to salvation, and the other is wicked and perverse, pushing us into damnation. But it is Iranian angelology that gives the guardian angel its most limpid and astonishing formulation. According to this doctrine, an angel called a *daena*, who has the form of a very beautiful young girl, presides over the birth of each man. The *daena* is the celestial archetype in whose likeness each individual has been created, as well as the silent witness who accompanies and observes us at every moment. And yet the angel's face changes over time. Like the picture of Dorian Gray, it is imperceptibly transformed with our every gesture, word, and thought. Thus, at the moment of death, the soul is met by its angel, which has been transfigured by the soul's conduct into either a more beautiful creature or a horrendous demon. It then whispers: "I am your *daena*, the one who has been formed by your thoughts, your words, and your deeds." In a vertiginous reversal, our life molds and outlines the archetype in whose image we are created.

To some extent we all come to terms with Genius, with what resides in us but does not belong to us. Each person's character is engendered by the way he attempts to turn away from Genius, to flee from him. Genius, to the extent that he has been avoided and left unexpressed, inscribes a grimace on Ego's face. An author's style — like the grace displayed by any creature — depends less on his genius than on the part of him that is deprived of genius, his character. That is why when we love someone we actually love neither his genius nor his character (and even less his ego) but his special manner of evading both of these poles, his rapid back-and-forth between genius and character. (For example, the childlike grace with which a certain poet in Naples gulped down ice cream in secret, or the awkward, shambling way a certain philosopher would pace the room as he spoke, stopping suddenly and staring at a distant corner of the ceiling.)

But for each person there comes a time when he must be separated from his Genius. It can be at night, unexpectedly, when at the sound of a group of people passing by he feels, without knowing why, that his god has abandoned him. Or perhaps we send Genius away in a moment of great lucidity, an extreme moment in which we know there is salvation but no longer want to be saved — as when in *The Tempest*, Prospero says to Ariel: "Be free." This is the moment when he relinquishes the spirit's charms and knows that the strength he has now is his own; it is the late and final stage when the old artist lays down his pen — and contemplates. What does he contemplate? Gestures: for the first time truly his own, devoid of every charm. No doubt life without Ariel loses its mystery, and yet somehow we know that now it can really belong to us; only now do we begin to live a purely human and earthly life, the life that did not keep its promises and, for that reason, can now give us infinitely more. This is exhausted and suspended time, the sudden penumbra in which we begin to forget about Genius; this is night fulfilled.[3] Did Ariel ever exist? What is that fading, distant music? Only the departure is true; only now does the very long unlearning of the self begin — before the gangling boy returns to take up his blushing glances one by one and, one by one, imperiously, his hesitations.

CHAPTER TWO

Magic and Happiness

Walter Benjamin once said that a child's first experience of the world is not his realization that "adults are stronger but rather that he cannot make magic."[1] The statement was made under the influence of a twenty-milligram dose of mescaline, but that does not make it any less salient. It is, in fact, quite likely that the invincible sadness that sometimes overwhelms children is born precisely from their awareness that they are incapable of magic. Whatever we can achieve through merit and effort, cannot make us truly happy. Only magic can do that. This did not escape the childlike genius of Mozart, who clearly indicated the secret solidarity between magic and happiness in a letter to Joseph Bullinger: "To Live respectably and to live happily are two very different things, and the latter will not be possible for me without some kind of magic; for this, something truly super-natural would have to happen."[2]

Like creatures in fables, children know that in order to be happy it is necessary to keep the genie in the bottle at one's side, and have the donkey that craps gold coins or the hen that lays golden eggs in one's house. And no matter what the situation, it is much more important to know the exact place and the right words to say than to take the trouble to reach a goal by honest means. Magic means precisely that no one can be worthy of happiness and that, as the ancients knew, any happiness commensurate with man is always hubris; it is always the result of arrogance and excess. But if someone succeeds in influencing fortune through trickery, if happiness depends not on what one is but on a magic walnut or an "Open sesame!" — then and only then can one consider oneself to be truly and blessedly happy.

This childlike wisdom, which affirms that happiness is not something that can be deserved, has always met with the objections of official morality. Take the words of Kant, the philosopher who was least capable of understanding the difference between living with dignity and living happily: "That in you which strives toward happiness is inclination, that which then limits this inclination to the condition of your first being worthy of happiness is your reason."[3] But we (or the child within us) wouldn't know what to do with a happiness of which we were worthy. What a disaster if a woman loved you because you deserved it! And how boring to receive happiness as the reward of work well done.

That the bond linking magic and happiness is not simply immoral, that it can indeed testify to a higher ethics, is shown in the ancient maxim that whoever realizes he is happy has already ceased to be so. This means that happiness has a paradoxical relationship with its subject. Someone who is happy cannot know that he is; the subject of happiness is not a subject per se and does not obtain the form of a consciousness or of a conscience, not even a good one. Here magic appears as an exception, the only one that allows someone to be happy and to know that he is. Whoever enjoys something through en-

chantment escapes from the hubris implicit in the consciousness of happiness, since, in a certain sense, the happiness that
he knows he possesses is not his. Thus when Zeus assumes the
likeness of Amphitryon and unites with the beautiful Alcmene,
he does not enjoy her as Zeus, nor even, despite appearances, as
Amphitryon. His enjoyment lies entirely in enchantment, and
only what has been obtained through the crooked paths of
magic can be enjoyed consciously and purely. Only someone
who is enchanted can say "I" with a smile, and the only happiness that is truly deserved is the one we could never dream of
deserving.

That is the ultimate reason for the precept that there is only one
way to achieve happiness on this earth: to believe in the divine
and not to aspire to reach it (there is an ironic variation of this
in a conversation between Franz Kafka and Gustav Janouch,
when Kafka affirms that there is plenty of hope — but not for
us).[4] This apparently ascetic thesis becomes intelligible only if
we understand the meaning of this "not for us." It means not
that happiness is reserved only for others (happiness is, precisely, for us) but that it awaits us only at the point where it was
not destined for us. That is: happiness can be ours only through
magic. At that point, when we have wrenched it away from fate,
happiness coincides entirely with our knowing ourselves to be
capable of magic, with the gesture we use to banish that childhood sadness once and for all.

If this is so, if there is no other happiness than feeling capable of
magic, then Kafka's enigmatic definition of magic becomes
clear. He writes that if we call life by its right name, it comes
forth, because "that is the essence of magic, which does not

create but summons."[5] This definition agrees with the ancient tradition scrupulously followed by kabbalists and necromancers, according to which magic is essentially a science of secret names. Each thing, each being, has in addition to its manifest name another, hidden name to which it cannot fail to respond. To be a magus means to know and evoke these archi-names. Hence the interminable discussions of names (diabolical or angelic) through which the necromancer ensures his mastery over spiritual powers. For him, the secret name is only the seal of his power of life and death over the creature that bears it.

But according to another, more luminous tradition, the secret name is not so much the cipher of the thing's subservience to the magus's speech as, rather, the monogram that sanctions its liberation from language. The secret name was the name by which the creature was called in Eden. When it is pronounced, every manifest name — the entire Babel of names — is shattered. That is why, according to this doctrine, magic is a call to happiness. The secret name is the gesture that restores the creature to the unexpressed. In the final instance, magic is not a knowledge of names but a gesture, a breaking free from the name. That is why a child is never more content than when he invents a secret language. His sadness comes less from ignorance of magic names than from his own inability to free himself from the name that has been imposed on him. No sooner does he succeed, no sooner does he invent a new name, than he holds in his hands the *laissez-passer* that grants him happiness. To have a name is to be guilty. And justice, like magic, is nameless. Happy, and without a name, the creature knocks at the gates of the land of the magi, who speak in gestures alone.

Chapter Three

Judgment Day

What quality fascinates and entrances me in the photographs I love? I believe it is this: for me, photography in some way captures the Last Judgment; it represents the world as it appears on the last day, the Day of Wrath. It is, of course, not a question of subject matter. I don't mean that the photographs I love are ones that represent something grave, serious, or even tragic. The photo can show any face, any object, or any event whatever. This is the case with photographers like Mario Dondero and Robert Capa, active journalists who practice what could be called photographic *flânerie*: walking without any goal and photographing everything that happens. But "everything that happens" — the faces of two women riding bicycles in Scotland, a shop window in Paris — is called forth, summoned to appear on Judgment Day.

There is one example that shows with absolute clarity how this has been true ever since the history of photography began. The daguerreotype *Boulevard du Temple* is very well known; it is considered the first photograph in which a human figure appears. The silver plate represents the Boulevard du Temple, photographed by Daguerre from the window of his studio at a busy moment in the middle of the day. The boulevard should be crowded with people and carriages, and yet, because the cameras of the period required an extremely long exposure time, absolutely nothing of this moving mass is visible. Nothing, that is, except a small black silhouette on the sidewalk in the lower left-hand corner of the photograph. A man stopped to have his shoes shined, and must have stood still for quite a while, with his leg slightly raised to place his foot on the shoeshiner's stool.

I could never have invented a more adequate image of the Last Judgment. The crowd of humans — indeed, all of humanity — is present, but it cannot be seen, because the judgment concerns a single person, a single life: precisely this one and no other. And when has that life, that person, been picked out, captured, and immortalized by the angel of the Last Judgment — who is also the angel of photography? While making the most banal and ordinary gesture, the gesture of having his shoes shined. In the supreme instant, man, each man, is given over forever to his smallest, most everyday gesture. And yet, thanks to the photographic lens, that gesture is now charged with the weight of an entire life; that insignificant or even silly moment collects and condenses in itself the meaning of an entire existence.

I believe there is a secret relationship between gesture and photography. The power of the gesture to summon and sum up entire orders of angelic powers resides in the photographic lens and has its locus, its opportune moment, in photography. Walter Benjamin once wrote that Julien Green represented his characters with a gesture charged with destiny, that he fixed them in the irrevocability of an infernal beyond.[1] I believe the hell in question here is a pagan, not Christian one. In Hades, the shades of the dead repeat the same gesture ad infinitum: Ixion turns on his wheel; the Danaides attempt in vain to carry water in a sieve. But this is not a punishment; the pagan shades cannot be equated with the damned. Here, eternal repetition is the cipher of an *apokatastasis*, the infinite recapitulation of an existence.

A good photographer knows how to grasp the eschatological nature of the gesture — without, however, taking anything away from the historicity or singularity of the photographed event. I am thinking of the wartime correspondence between Dondero and Capa, or of the photograph of East Berlin taken from the roof of the Reichstag the day before the fall of the Berlin Wall. Or of the (rightly famous) photograph that Dondero took of the *nouveau roman* authors — Nathalie Sarraute, Samuel Beckett, Claude Simon, Alain Robbe-Grillet — outside the offices of the Editions de Minuit in 1959. All these photographs contain an unmistakable historical index, an indelible date, and yet, thanks to the special power of the gesture, this index now refers to another time, more actual and more urgent that any chronological time.

But there is another aspect of the photographs I love that I am compelled to mention. It has to do with a certain exigency: the subject shown in the photo demands something from us. The concept of exigency is particularly important and must not be confused with factual necessity. Even if the person photographed is completely forgotten today, even if his or her name has been erased forever from human memory — or, indeed, precisely because of this — that person and that face demand their name; they demand not to be forgotten.

Benjamin must have had something like this in mind when, referring to the photographs of David Octavius Hill, he wrote that the image of the fishwife gives rise to an exigency, a demand for the name of that woman who was once alive.[2] It is perhaps because they could not bear this mute apostrophe that the viewers of the first daguerreotypes had to turn away — they felt they were being watched by the people portrayed. (In the room where I work, on a piece of furniture next to my desk, there sits a photograph — a rather well-known one, in fact — that shows the face of a young Brazilian girl, who seems to stare harshly at me. I know with absolute certainty that she is and will be my judge, today as on the final judgment day.)

Dondero once expressed reservations about two photographers he admired; Henri Cartier-Bresson and Sebastião Salgado. In the first he saw an excess of geometrical construction; in the second an excess of aesthetic perfection. He opposed both of them with his own conception of the human face as a story to be told or a geography to be explored. I feel the same way: the photographic exigency that interpellates us has nothing aesthetic about it. It is, rather, a demand for redemption. The photograph is always more than an image: it is the site of a gap, a sublime breach between the sensible and the intelligible, between copy and reality, between a memory and a hope.

Christian theologians concerned with the resurrection of the flesh repeatedly asked themselves whether the body would be resuscitated in the condition it happened to be in at the moment of death (perhaps old, bald, missing a leg) or in the integrity of its youth. But they were never able to find a satisfactory answer. Origen cut short these endless discussions by

26

claiming that the resurrection concerns the form of the body, its *eidos*, rather than the body itself. Photography is, in this sense, a prophecy of the glorious body.

It is well known that Proust was obsessed with photography and that he went to great lengths to obtain photographs of the people he loved and admired. In response to his insistent requests for a portrait, one of the boys he had fallen in love with when he was twenty-two years old, Edgar Auber, finally gave one to Proust. On the back of the photograph, Auber wrote, by way of dedication (and in English): *Look at my face: my name is Might Have Been; I am also called No More, Too Late, Farewell.* A pretentious dedication, certainly, but it perfectly expresses the exigency that animates every photograph and grasps the real that is always in the process of being lost, in order to render it possible once again.

Photography demands that we remember all this, and photographs testify to all those lost names, like a Book of Life that the new angel of the apocalypse — the angel of photography — holds in his hands at the end of all days, that is, every day.

CHAPTER FOUR

The Assistants

In Kafka's novels, we encounter creatures who are referred to as *Gehilfen*, "assistants" or "helpers." But help seems to be the last thing they are able to give. They have no knowledge, no skills, and no "equipment"; they never do anything but engage in foolish behavior and childish games; they are "pests" and even sometimes "cheeky" and "lecherous." As for their appearance, they are so similar that they can only be told apart by their names (Arthur, Jeremiah); they are "as alike as snakes." And yet they are attentive observers, "quick" and "supple"; they have sparkling eyes and, in contrast to their childish ways, the adult faces, "of students almost" with long, thick beards. Someone, it's not clear who, has assigned them to us, and it isn't easy to get them off our backs. In sum, "we don't know who they are" — perhaps they are "emissaries" from the enemy (which would explain why they do nothing but lie in wait and watch). But they look like angels, messengers who do not know the content of the letters they must deliver, but whose smile, whose look, whose very posture "seems like a message."

Each of us has known such creatures, whom Walter Benjamin defines as "crepuscular" and incomplete, similar to the *gandharva*s of the Indian sages, who are half celestial genie, half demon. "None has a firm place in the world, or firm, inalienable outlines. There is not one that is not either rising or falling, none that is not trading its qualities with its enemy or neighbor; none that has not completed its period of time and yet is unripe, none that is not deeply exhausted and yet is only at the beginning of a long existence."[1] More intelligent and gifted than our other friends, always intent on notions and projects for which they seem to have all the necessary virtues, they still do not succeed in finishing anything and are generally idle [senz'opera]. They embody the type of eternal student or swindler who ages badly and who must be left behind in the end, even if it is against our wishes. And yet something about them, an inconclusive gesture, an unforeseen grace, a certain mathematical boldness in judgment and taste, a certain air of nimbleness in their limbs or words — all these features indicate that they belong to a complementary world and allude to a lost citizenship or an inviolable elsewhere. In this sense, they give us help, even though we can't quite tell what sort of help it is. It could consist precisely in the fact that they cannot be helped, or in their stubborn insistence that "there is nothing to be done for us." For that very reason, we know, in the end, that we have somehow betrayed them.

Perhaps because children are incomplete beings, children's literature is full of assistants and helpers, parallel and approximate beings who are too small or too large, gnomes, wraiths, good giants, fairies, and capricious genies, talking crickets and snails, donkeys who defecate gold coins, and other enchanted creatures who miraculously appear to whisk away the good little princess or Jean Sans Peur from danger. These figures are forgotten by the narrator at the end of the story when the protagonists go on to live happily ever after. We learn nothing more about them, this unclassifiable "crew" to whom, at bottom, the main characters owe everything. Try asking Prospero — after he has abandoned all his charms and returned with the other humans to his duchy — what life is like without Ariel.

A perfect type of helper is Pinocchio, the marvelous puppet that Geppetto wants to make so that he can travel the world with him and thus earn a "crust of bread and a glass of wine."[2] Neither dead nor alive, half golem and half robot, always ready to yield to temptation one moment and then to promise "to be good from now on," this eternal archetype of seriousness and of the grace of the inhuman simply "stretches out his legs" at a certain point and dies most shamefully, without ever becoming a boy. (This is in the first version of the story, before the author thought it necessary to add an edifying conclusion.) Another assistant is Lampwick, with his "scrawny little frame, just like the new wick of a night-lamp," who describes Funland to his companions and bursts out laughing when he realizes that Pinocchio has sprouted a pair of donkey's ears.[3] Robert Walser's assistants are made of the very same stuff — these figures who are irreparably and stubbornly busy collaborating on work that is utterly superfluous, not to say indescribable. If they study — and they seem to study very hard — it is in order to become big fat zeros. And why should they bother to help with anything the world takes seriously? After all, it's nothing but madness. They prefer to take walks. And if they encounter a dog or some living creature on their walks, they whisper: "I have nothing to give you, dear animal; I would gladly give you something, if only I had it." Nevertheless, in the end, they lie down in a meadow to weep bitterly over their "stupid greenhorn's existence."

One also finds assistants and helpers among the world of in-animate things. Everyone keeps certain useless and somewhat shameful objects — half souvenirs, half talismans — which one wouldn't renounce for anything in the world. Such an object could be an old plaything that has survived the ravages of childhood, a pencil box that still retains a lost scent, or a tiny T-shirt that we continue to keep, for no reason, in the drawer meant for men's shirts. For Charles Foster Kane, the sled called Rosebud must have been something of this sort. Or, think of the Maltese falcon, which for its pursuers turns out to be "the stuff that dreams are made of." Or, there is also the scooter engine that becomes a cream whipper in Alfred Sohn-Rethel's magnificent description of Naples. Where do they, these helper-objects, these testimonies to an unavowed Eden go in the end? Is there some storehouse for them, some ark in which they will be collected for eternity, like the *genizah* in which Jews keep old, illegible books, just in case the name of God is written in one of them?

Chapter 366 of *The Meccan Revelations*, the masterwork of the great Sufi Ibn al-ʻArabi, is dedicated to "the helpers of the Messiah."[4] These helpers (*wuzara'*, the plural of *wazir*; the vizier we have encountered so many times in *The Thousand and One Nights*) are men who, in profane time, already possess the characteristics of messianic time: they already belong to the last day. Curiously — but perhaps for this very reason — they are chosen from among non-Arabs; they are foreigners among the Arabs, even if they speak their language. The *Mahdi*, the mes-siah who comes at the end of time, needs his helpers, who are in some ways his guides, even if they are, in truth, only the per-sonifications of the qualities or "stations" of his wisdom. "The

Mahdi makes his decisions and judgments on the basis of consultation with them, since they are the true Knowers who really know what is there in the divine Reality."[5] Thanks to his helpers, the *Mahdi* can understand the language of the animals and can extend his justice over both men and jinn. One of the qualities of the helper is, in fact, that he is a "translator" (*mutarjim*) of the language of God, which he renders into the language of men. According to Ibn al-'Arabi, the entire world is in fact nothing other than a translation of the divine language, and the helpers are, in this sense, the operators of an incessant theophany, a continuous revelation. Another quality of the assistant is his "penetrating vision," which recognizes the "men of the invisible realm," that is, the angels and the other messengers who hide in human and animal forms.

But how can one recognize these helpers, these translators? If they hide among the faithful as foreigners, who will have the vision capable of distinguishing the visionaries?

An intermediate creature who exists between the *wazir* and Kafka's assistants is the little hunchback that Benjamin evokes in his childhood memories.[6] This "tenant of the distorted life" is not just the cipher of childish clumsiness, nor the trickster who steals the glass from someone who wants to drink and the prayer from someone who wants to pray. Rather, his appearance makes it so that whoever looks at him "can no longer pay attention" to himself or to the little man. The hunchback is, in fact, the representative of the forgotten; he presents himself in order to lay claim to the aspect of oblivion that resides in every thing. This share of oblivion has something to do with the end of time, just as carelessness is a precursor to redemption. Distortion, the hump, and clumsiness are the forms things take in oblivion. What we have always already forgotten is the Kingdom, we who live "as if we were not the Kingdom." When the messiah comes, the distorted will be straightened, the obstacle will become easy, and the forgotten will be remembered of its own accord. For it is said, "for them and their kind, the incomplete and the inept, to them hope will be given."

The idea that the Kingdom is present in profane time in sinister and distorted forms, that the elements of the final state are hidden precisely in what today appears despicable and derisory, that shame, in sum, secretly has something to do with glory, is a profound messianic theme. Everything that now appears debased and worthless to us is the currency we will have to redeem on the last day. And we will be guided toward salvation precisely by the companion who has lost his way. It is his face that we will recognize in the angel who sounds the trumpet or who carelessly drops the Book of Life from his hands. The bead of light that emerges from our defects and our little abjections is nothing other than redemption. In this sense, the naughty schoolmates who passed the first pornographic pictures to us under their school desks, or the sordid closet in which someone showed us his or her nudity for the first time, were also assistants. The assistants are our unfulfilled desires, the ones we do not confess even to ourselves. On the day of judgment, they will come smiling toward us like Arthur and Jeremiah. That day, someone will count off our blushes like a collection notice for paradise. To reign does not mean to fulfill. It means that the unfulfilled is what remains.

The assistant is the figure of what is lost. Or, rather, of our relationship to what is lost. This relationship concerns everything that, in both collective and individual life, comes to be forgotten at every moment. It concerns the unending mass of what becomes irrevocably lost. Throughout our lives, the measure of oblivion and ruin, the ontological waste that we carry in ourselves, far exceeds the small mercy of our memories and our consciousness. But this formless chaos of the forgotten that accompanies us like a silent golem is neither inert nor inefficacious. On the contrary, it influences us just as much as our conscious memories, although in a different way. It is a force and almost an apostrophe of the forgotten that, although it can neither be measured in terms of consciousness nor accumulated as a patrimony, insistently governs the hierarchy of all knowledge and all consciousness. What is lost demands not to be remembered and fulfilled but to remain forgotten or lost and therefore, for that reason alone, unforgettable. The assistant is at home in all this. He spells out the text of the unforgettable and translates it into the language of deaf-mutes. Hence his obstinate gesticulations coupled with his impassive mime's face. Hence, too, his irreducible ambiguity. For the unforgettable is articulated only in parody. The place of song is empty. On every side and all around us, the assistants are busy preparing the Kingdom.

CHAPTER FIVE

Parody

In her novel *Arturo's Island*, Elsa Morante presents a concealed meditation on parody that very likely makes a decisive statement about her poetics. The term *Parody* (with a capital P) appears rather unexpectedly as an insulting epithet for one of the central characters of the novel, Wilhelm Gerace, the idol and father of Arturo, the story's narrator.[1] When Arturo hears the word for the first time (or, rather, when he translates it from the secret language of whistles that he believes he alone shared with his father), he is uncertain of its meaning. In order not to forget it, he mentally repeats it to himself as he returns home, where he consults a dictionary and finds the following definition: "Imitation of someone else's verse in which what is serious in the other becomes ridiculous, comic, or grotesque."[2]

This intrusion of a definition from a manual of rhetoric into a literary text cannot be a matter of chance. Especially since the term reappears shortly before the end of the novel, in an episode that contains the final revelation that leads to Arturo's separation from his father, the island, and his childhood. The revelation is this: "Your father is a Parody!"[3] Recalling the dictionary definition, Arturo futilely searches the thin, gracious face of his father for the comic or grotesque features that might justify the epithet. A little later, he realizes that his father is in

37

love with the man who insulted him. The name of a literary genre is here the cipher of an inversion involving the object of desire rather than the transposition of the serious into the comic. It could also be said that the character's homosexuality is a cipher that indicates he is nothing other than a symbol for the literary genre with which the narrative voice (which is obviously also the voice of the author) has fallen in love. In accordance with a specific allegorical intention, for which it is not difficult to find precedents in medieval texts but which is almost unique in the modern novel, Elsa Morante has made a literary genre — parody — the protagonist of her book. Considered from this perspective, *Arturo's Island* appears as the story of the author's desperate and childish love for a literary object that seems highly serious and almost legendary in the beginning, but that reveals itself to be accessible only in a parodic form in the end.

The definition of parody that Arturo finds in the dictionary is a relatively modern one. It comes from a rhetorical tradition whose exemplary crystallization appears at the end of the sixteenth century in the work of Giulio Cesare Scaligero, who devotes an entire chapter of his *Poetics* to parody. Scaligero's definition provided the model that dominated the tradition for centuries:

> Just as Satire derives from Tragedy and Mime from Comedy, so does Parody derive from Rhapsody. Indeed, when the rhapsodes interrupted their recitation, performers entered who, out of playfulness and in order to spur the souls of the listeners, inverted and overturned everything that had come before.... For that reason, these songs were called *paroidous*, because alongside

38

and in addition to the serious argument, they inserted other ridiculous things. Parody is therefore an inverted Rhapsody that transposes the sense into something ridiculous by changing the words. It was similar to Epirrhema and Parabasis.

Scaligero was one of the sharpest minds of his age. His definition contains certain important elements, such as the references to the Homeric poets (rhapsody) and to comic parabasis, to which we will return in a moment. It also establishes the two canonical features of parody: the dependence on a preexistent model that is subsequently transformed from something serious into something comic, and the preservation of formal elements into which new and incongruous contents are introduced. From here it is a short step to modern manuals' definition, such as the one that Arturo finds so thought provoking. Medieval sacred parody such as the *missa potatorum* and the *Coena Cypriani*, which introduce crude contents into the liturgy of the mass or into the text of the Bible, are in this sense perfect examples of parody.

The classical world, however, was familiar with another, more ancient, meaning that situated parody in the sphere of musical technique. This definition made a distinction between song and speech, *melos* and *logos*. In Greek music, in fact, melody was originally supposed to correspond to the rhythm of speech. In the case of the recitation of the Homeric poems, when this traditional link is broken and the rhapsodes begin to introduce discordant melodies, it is said that they are singing *para tēn ōidēn*, against (or beside) the song. Aristotle informs us that the first to introduce parody into rhapsody in this sense was Hegemon of Thasos.[4] We know that his mode of recitation provoked irrepressible fits of laughter among the Athenians. It is said that the cither player Oinopas introduced parody into lyric poetry also by separating the music from the words. The split between song and language appears complete in Callias, who composed a song in which words give way to the recitation of the alphabet (beta alpha, beta eta, and so on).

According to this more ancient meaning of the term, then, parody designates the rupture of the "natural" bond between music and language, the separation of song from speech. Or, conversely, of speech from song. It is, in fact, precisely this parodic loosening of the traditional link between music and *logos* that made possible the birth of the art of prose with Gorgias. Breaking this link liberates a *para*, a space beside, in which prose takes its place. This means that literary prose carries in itself the mark of its separation from song. The "obscure song" that, according to Cicero, is felt in a prose speech (*est autem etiam in dicendo quidam cantus obscurior*) is, in this sense, a lament for this lost music, for the disappearance of the natural place of song.[5]

The notion that parody constitutes the stylistic key to Morante's world is certainly nothing new. Reference has been made in this respect to "serious parody."

The concept of "serious parody" is obviously contradictory, not because parody is not a serious matter (indeed, at times it is extremely serious) but because it cannot claim to be identified with the parodied work; it also cannot deny being necessarily beside the song (*para-ōiden*), and thus it cannot deny its own not taking place. However, there may be great seriousness in the reasons that drive the parodist to renounce a direct representation of his or her object. For Morante, these reasons are as evident as they are substantial: the object that she must describe — the innocent life, that is, life outside history — is rigorously unnarratable. The precocious explanation that she gives of it in a fragment from 1950 — an explanation borrowed from the Judeo-Christian myth — is definitive for her poetics: man was driven from Eden; he lost his own place and, together with the animals, was thrown into a history that does not belong to him. The very object of narration is, in this sense, "parodic," that is, out of place, and the writer can only repeat and mimic the intimate parody of this object. Since she wants to evoke the unnarratable, she must necessarily resort to childish means and to "novelistic vices", as the author suggests at the end of the book in one of the rare moments when she takes over Arturo's voice. Morante must therefore count on well-informed readers to fill in and supplement, as it were, the unbearably stereotypical and parodic quality of many of her characters who, like Useppe and Arturo himself, seem to come from illustrated children's books. Her narratives are half *Cuore* and half *Treasure Island*, half fable and half mystery.[6]

The notion that life can be presented in literature only in terms of a mystery is a theorem that is very fitting for Morante ("Thus life remained a mystery," says Arturo before his last departure). We know that in the case of the pagan mysteries the inititated attended theatrical events that involved toys: tops, pinecones, mirrors (an ill-intentioned source defines them as *puerilia ludicra*). It is useful to reflect on the childish aspects of every mystery and on the intimate solidarity that binds mystery to parody. In approaching a mystery, one can offer nothing but a parody; any other attempt to evoke it falls into bad taste and bombast. In this sense, we can call the liturgy of the mass, the representation par excellence of the modern mystery, parodic. This is supported by the countless medieval sacred parodies which exhibit such a lack of profanatory intention they have been preserved by the faithful hands of the monks. Faced with mystery, artistic creation can only become caricature, in the sense in which Nietzsche, on the lucid threshold of madness, wrote to Jacob Burckhardt: "I am God, I made this caricature; I would rather be a professor in Basel than God, but I cannot push my egoism that far."[7] It is through a sort of probity that the artist, feeling himself unable to push his egoism to the point of wanting to represent the unnarratable, assumes parody as the very form of mystery.

The institution of parody as the form of mystery perhaps defines the most extreme of the parodic countertexts of the Middle Ages, in which the aura of mystery at the center of chivalric intention is converted into the most unrestrained scatology. I am referring to *Audigier*, a poem in Old French composed sometime around the end of the twelfth century and preserved in a single manuscript. The genealogy and entire existence of its antihero and protagonist are inscribed within a constellation that is resolutely cloacal. His father, Turgibus, is lord of Cocuce, "a soft country / where the people are in shit up to their elbows. / I got there by swimming through a stream of crap, / and I couldn't get out again through any other hole." Concerning this noble gentleman, of whom Audigier shows himself to be a worthy heir, we know that "when he shit all over his clothes, / he stuck his fingers in the crap, and sucked on them." But the true parodic nucleus of the poem is found in the imitation of the ceremony of knightly investiture, which unfolds in a dung pit, and, above all, in the repeated struggles with the enigmatic old Grinberge. These struggles unfailingly end in a sort of mock scatalogical sacrament, which Audigier undergoes like a "true gentleman":

Grinberge a decouvert et cul et con
et sor le vis li ert a estupon;
du cul li chiet la merde a grant foison.
Quans Audigier se siet sor un fumier envers,
Et Grinberge sor lui qui li froie les ners.
ii. foiz li fist baiser son cul ainz qu'il fust ters.

[Grinberge uncovered her ass and cunt
and squatted down over his face.
Shit fell from her ass in great profusion.
While Audigier lay down on a dungheap,
Grinberge sat on him and rubbed his ankles.
Twice she had him kiss her ass until it was wiped cleaned.][8]

This is less a return to the womb or an initiate's trial, both of which have precedents in folklore, than an audacious inversion of the stakes involved in the chivalric quest and, more generally, of the object of courtly love, which is abruptly taken from the prestigious sphere of the sacred to the profane site of the dunghill. It is even possible that the unknown author of the poem is thus doing nothing other than making crudely explicit a parodic intention already present in chivalric literature and love poetry: to confuse and render indiscernible the threshold that separates the sacred and the profane, love and sexuality, the sublime and the base.

The poetic dedication that opens *Arturo's Island* establishes a correspondence between the "small celestial island" that is

the setting of the novel (childhood?) and limbo. But this correspondence has a bitter codicil: "*Outside limbo there is no Elysium.*"⁹ Bitter, because it implies that happiness can exist only
in a parodic form (as limbo, not as Elysium — and this is yet
another exchange of places).

A reading of the theological treatises on limbo shows, beyond any doubt, that the Church Fathers conceived of the
"first circle" as a parody of both paradise and hell, of beatitude
as well as damnation. It is a parody of paradise insofar as it contains creatures who, like the blessed, are innocent and yet carry
in themselves the original stain — children who died before
being baptized or righteous pagans who could not have known.
The most ironically parodic moment, however, concerns hell.
According to the theologians, the punishment an inhabitant of
limbo undergoes cannot be an afflictive one, like that reserved
for the damned, but must be a privative one, consisting in a
perpetual inability to perceive God. This lack, though, which
constitutes the first of the infernal punishments, does not
cause the residents of limbo pain, as it does the damned. Since
they have only natural consciousness and not the supernatural
one that derives from baptism, the lack of the highest good
does not cause them the slightest regret. Thus the creatures of
limbo convert the greatest punishment into a natural joy, and
this joy is certainly an extreme and special form of parody.
Hence, however, the veil of sadness that covers the inviolate
island "like some grey thing," as Morante sees it. The "house of
the kids," whose very name evokes the children's limbo, contains, along with the memory of the homosexual orgies of the
man from Amalfi, a parody of innocence.

In a certain sense, the entire tradition of Italian literature
stands under the sign of parody. Guglielmo Gorni has shown

how parody (here too a serious form) is an essential constituent of Dante's style, which aims to produce a double that
is almost equal in dignity to the passages of sacred scripture
that it reproduces.[10] But the presence of a parodic strain in Italian literature goes even deeper. All poets are enamored of their
language. But usually something is revealed to them through
the language that enraptures them and occupies them so completely: the divine, love, the good, the city, nature.... With the
Italian poets — at least beginning at a certain moment — something peculiar happens: they become enamored with their language alone, and this language reveals nothing to them but
itself. And this is the cause — or perhaps the consequence — of
something else that is peculiar, namely that the Italian poets
hate their language as much as they love it. That is why, in their
case, parody does not simply insert more or less comic content
into a serious form, but parodies language itself, so to speak. It
thus introduces a split into language — or discovers a split in
language (and therefore in love), which amounts to the same
thing. The persistent bilingualism of Italian literary culture
(the split between Latin and the vulgate and, later, with the
gradual decline of Latin, between the dead language and the
living language, literary language and dialect) certainly has a
parodic function in this sense. Whether in a poetically constitutive mode, like the opposition between grammar and the
mother tongue in Dante, in elegiac and pedantic forms, as in
the *Hypnerotomachia Poliphili*, or in crude forms, as in Folengo,
what is essential in each case is the ability to introduce into
language a tension which parody uses to install, as it were, its
central power source.

It is not difficult to see the results of this tension in twenti-
eth-century literature. Parody goes from being a literary genre

to the very structure of the linguistic medium in which litera-ture expresses itself. Writers who mobilize this dualism as a sort of "discord" internal to language (Carlo Emilio Gadda and Giorgio Manganelli) can be contrasted with writers who, in verse or in prose, parodically celebrate the nonplace of song (Giovanni Pascoli and, in a different way, Elsa Morante and Tommaso Landolfi). In both cases, however, it is taken for granted that one sings — or speaks — only alongside language or song.

If the presupposition of the object's unattainability is essential to parody, then the poetry of the troubadours and the *stilnovisti* contains an indubitable parodic intention. It reflects the simul-taneously complicated and childish character of its formality. *L'amor de lonh* is a parody that guarantees the separation of the object from that with which it seeks to be united. This is also true on the linguistic level. Metrical preciosity and *trobar clus* establish differences of level and polarities in language that transform signification into a field of unresolved tensions.

But polar tensions also emerge on the erotic plane. It is always astonishing to find an obscene and burlesque drive along-side a more refined spirituality, often in the same person (the exemplary case is Daniel Arnaut, whose obscene *sirventes* never ceases to raise difficult problems for scholars). The poet, obses-sively occupied with keeping the love object at a distance, lives in a symbiotic relationship with the parodist, who systemati-cally inverts his intention.

Modern love poetry is born under the ambiguous sign of parody. Petrarch's *Canzoniere*, which resolutely turns away from the troubadour tradition, is an attempt to save poetry from parody. His formula is both simple and effective: with

46

regard to language, an integral monolinguism (Latin and popular language are separate to the point of no longer communicating, and the differences in meter are abolished) plus the elimination of the loved object's unattainability (obviously not in a realistic sense, but by transforming the unattainable into a cadaver — indeed, into a specter). The dead aura [*l'aura morta*] becomes the proper object of poetry, and one that it is impossible to parody. *Exit parodia. Incipit literatura.*

Repressed parody reappears, however, in a pathological form. The fact that the first biography of Laura was written by an ancestor of the Marquis de Sade, who includes her in his genealogy, is not merely an ironic coincidence. It announces the work of the Divine Marquis as the most implacable revocation of the *Canzoniere*. Pornography, which maintains the intangibility of its own fantasy in the same gesture with which it brings it closer — in a mode that is unbearable to look at — is the eschatological form of parody.

The critic Franco Fortini suggests applying the formula "serious parody" not only to Morante but to Pasolini as well. He recommends that we read Pasolini's late works in close proximity with those of Morante. The suggestion could be developed further. At one point, Pasolini not only carried on a dialogue with Morante (whom he ironically calls Basilissa in his poetry), but also more or less consciously parodied her work. Indeed, Pasolini, too, began with a linguistic parody (his Friulian poems, his incongruous use of the Roman dialect) in the footsteps of Morante. With his shift to the cinema, though, he displaced the parody onto its contents, giving it the weight of a metaphysical signification. Like language, life bears a split within itself (the analogy is not surprising, if we consider the theological equation between life and the word that profoundly marks the Christian world). The poet can live "without the comforts of religion" (to quote the title of an unpublished novel by Morante) but not without those of parody. Morante's cult of Umberto Saba corresponds to Pasolini's cult of Sandro Penna; the "long celebration of vitality in Morante" to the trilogy of life. The angelic little boys who must save the world correspond to the sanctification of Ninetto. In both cases, there is something unrepresentable in the very foundation of parody. And, finally, pornography appears here too in its apocalyptic function. From this perspective, it would not be illegitimate to read Pasolini's *Salò* as a parody of Morante's *History*.[11]

Parody maintains a special relationship with fiction, which has always constituted the distinctive trait of literature. One of the most beautiful poems in Morante's collection *Alibi* is devoted to fiction (and she knew that she was a master of fiction); it announces and condenses its musical theme: "Di te, finzione, mi cingo, fatua veste" ["With you, fiction, fatuous dress, I adorn myself"].[12] And it has been pointed out that, according to Pasolini, Morante's language itself is pure fiction (it "pretends that Italian exists"). In truth, parody not only does not coincide with fiction, but constitutes its polar opposite. This is because, unlike fiction, parody does not call into question the reality of its object; indeed, this object is so intolerably real for parody that it becomes necessary to keep it at a distance. To fiction's "as if," parody opposes its drastic "this is too much" (or "as if not"). Thus, if fiction defines the essence of literature, parody holds itself, so to speak, on the threshold of literature, stubbornly suspended between reality and fiction, between word and thing.

Perhaps there is no better place to grasp the affinity — as well as the distance — between these two symmetrical poles of creation than in the passage that leads from Beatrice to Laura. By allowing the object of his love to die, Dante certainly takes a step beyond the poetry of the troubadours. But his gesture remains parodic: the death of Beatrice is a parody that, by detaching the name from the mortal creature who bears it, is able to gather up its beatific essence. Hence the absolute lack of mourning and, in the end, the triumph of love rather than death. Laura's death, however, is the death of the parodic constitution of the love object for the troubadours and the *stilnovisti*. The object henceforth becomes only an "aura," only *flatus vocis*.

In this sense, writers distinguish themselves according to the way in which they inscribe themselves into one of two great classes: parody and fiction, Beatrice and Laura. But intermediate solutions are possible as well: one can parody fiction (which is Elsa Morante's vocation), or one can feign parody (which is the gesture of Manganelli and Landolfi).

If we pursue the metaphysical vocation of parody further, taking its gesture to an extreme, we can say that it presupposes a dual tension in being. In other words, the parodic split in language would necessarily correspond to a duplication of being — ontology would correspond to a paraontology. Alfred Jarry once defined his beloved child "pataphysics," as the science of what is added on to metaphysics. In the same way, one can say that parody is the theory — and practice — of that in language and in being which is beside itself — or, the being-beside-itself of every being and every discourse. Just as metaphysics is impossible — at least for modern thought — except as the parodic opening of a space alongside sensible experience (but a space that must remain rigorously empty), parody is a notoriously impracticable terrain, in which the traveler constantly knocks against limits and aporias that he cannot avoid but that he also cannot escape.

If ontology is the more or less felicitous relationship between language and world, then parody, as paraontology, expresses language's inability to reach the thing and the impossibility of the thing finding its own name. The space of parody — which is literature — is therefore necessarily and theologically marked by mourning and by the distorted grimace (just as the space of logic is marked by silence). And yet, in this way, parody attests to what seems to be the only possible truth of language.

At a certain point in his definition of parody, Scaligero mentions parabasis. In the technical language of Greek comedy, parabasis (or *parekbasis*) designates the moment when the actor exits the scene and the chorus turns directly to the spectators. In order to do this, in order to speak to the audience, the chorus moves over (*parabaino*) to the part of the stage called the *logeion*, the place of discourse.

In the gesture of parabasis, the representation is dissolved and actors and spectators, author and audience exchange roles. Here, the tension between stage and reality is relaxed and parody encounters what is perhaps its only resolution. Parabasis is an *Aufhebung* of parody — both a transgression and a completion. For this reason, Friedrich Schlegel, always attentive to every possible way of ironically surpassing art, sees parabasis as the point where theater goes beyond itself and approaches the novel, the Romantic form par excellence. The staged dialogue — intimately and parodically divided — opens a space off to the side (which is physically represented by the *logeion*) and thus becomes nothing more than an exchange, simply a human conversation.

Likewise, in literature, when the narrative voice turns to the reader, as in the famous apostrophes of the poet to the reader, this is a parabasis, an interruption of parody. It will be necessary to reflect, from this perspective, on the eminent function of parabasis in the modern novel, from Cervantes to Morante. Called forth and carried away from his place and his position, the reader accedes not to the place of the author but to a sort of space between worlds. If parody, the split between song and speech and between language and world, commemorates in reality the absence of a proper place for human speech, in parabasis this heart-wrenching atopia becomes, for a moment, less painful and is canceled out into a homeland [*si cancella in patria*], as it were. As Arturo says of his island: "I would rather pretend [*fingere*] that it doesn't exist. So I'd better not look until the moment when it can't be seen any longer. You tell me when that moment has come."[13]

CHAPTER SIX

Desiring

There is nothing simpler and more human than to desire. Why, then, are our desires unavowable for us? Why is it so difficult for us to put them into words? It is so difficult, in fact, that we end up hiding them, constructing a crypt for them somewhere within ourselves, where they remain embalmed, suspended and waiting.

We are unable to put our desires into language because we have imagined them. In reality, the crypt contains only images, like a picture book for children who do not yet know how to read, like the *Imagerie d'Epinal* of an illiterate people. The body of desires is an image. And what is unavowable in desire is the image we have made of it for ourselves.

To communicate one's desires to someone without images is brutal. To communicate one's images without one's desires is tedious (like recounting one's dreams or one's travels). But both of these are easy to do. To communicate the imagined desires and the desired images, on the other hand, is a more difficult task. And that is why we put it off until later. Until the moment when we begin to understand that desire will remain forever unfulfilled — and that this unavowed desire is ourselves, forever prisoners in the crypt.

The messiah comes for our desires. He separates them from images in order to fulfill them. Or rather, in order to show they have already been fulfilled. Whatever we have imagined, we have already had. There remain the (unfulfillable) images of what is already fulfilled. With fulfilled desires, he constructs hell; with unfulfillable images, limbo. And with imagined desire, with the pure word, the beatitude of paradise.

CHAPTER SEVEN

Special Being

Medieval philosophers were fascinated by mirrors. They inquired in particular into the nature of the images that appear in them: What is the being, or rather the nonbeing, of these images? Are they bodies or nonbodies, substances or accidents? Should they be identified with colors, with light, or with shadow? Are they endowed with local movement? And how does the mirror receive their form?

Certainly, the being of images must be very peculiar. If they were simply body or substance, how could they occupy the space already occupied by the body of the mirror? And if their place is the mirror, would we not also be displacing the images by displacing the mirror?

First of all, the image is not a substance but an accident that is found in the mirror, not as in a place but as in a subject (*quod est in speculo ut in subiecto*). For medieval philosophers, being in a subject is the mode of being assumed by what is without substance, that is, what exists not in itself but in something other than itself. (Given the proximity between the image and the experience of love, it is not surprising that both Dante and Cavalcanti were led to define love in the same way: as an "accident without substance.")

Two characteristics are derived from the insubstantial nature of the image. Since the image is not a substance, it does not possess any continuous reality and cannot be described as moving by means of any local movement. Rather, it is generated at every moment according to the movement or the presence of the one who contemplates it: "Just as light is always created anew according to the presence of the illuminator, so do we say that the image in the mirror is generated each time according to the presence of the one who looks."

The being of the image is a continuous generation (*semper nova generatur*), a being [*essere*] of generation and not of substance. Each moment, it is created anew, like the angels who, according to the Talmud, sing the praises of God and immediately sink into nothingness.

The second characteristic of the image is that it cannot be determined according to the category of quantity; it is not, properly speaking, a form or an image but rather the "*aspect* of an image or of a form" (*species imaginis et formae*). In itself, it cannot be described as long or wide, but instead as "having only the aspect of length and width." The dimensions of the image are therefore not measurable quantities but merely aspects or *species*, modes of being and "habits" (*habitus vel dispositiones*). This characteristic — being able to refer only to a "habit" or an ethos — is the most interesting signification of the expression "being in a subject." What is in a subject has the form of a *species*, a usage, a gesture. It is never a thing, but always and only a "kind of thing" [*specie di cosa*].

The Latin term *species*, which means "appearance," "aspect," or "vision," derives from a root signifying "to look, to see." This root is also found in *speculum* (mirror), *spectrum* (image, ghost), *perspicuus* (transparent, clearly seen), *speciosus* (beautiful, giving itself to be seen), *specimen* (example, sign), and *spectaculum* (spectacle). In philosophical terminology, *species* was used to translate the Greek *eidos* (as *genus* was used to translate *genos*); hence the sense the term takes on in natural science (animal or plant species) and in the language of commerce, where the term signifies "commodities" (particularly in the sense of drugs and spices) and, later, money (*espèces*).

The image is a being whose essence is to be a *species*, a visibility or an appearance. A being is special if its essence coincides with its being given to be seen, with its aspect.

Special being is absolutely insubstantial. It does not have a proper place, but it occurs in a subject and is in this sense like a *habitus* or a mode of being, like the image in a mirror.

The *species* of each thing is its visibility, that is, its pure intelligibility. A being is special if it coincides with its own becoming visible, with its own revelation.

The mirror is the place where we discover that we have an image and, at the same time, that this image can be separate from us, that our *species* or *imago* does not belong to us. Between the perception of the image and the recognition of oneself in it, there is a gap, which the medieval poets called love. In this sense, Narcissus's mirror is the source of love, the fierce and shocking realization that the image is and is not our image.

If the gap is eliminated, if one recognizes oneself in the image but without also being misrecognized and loved in it — if only for an instant — it means no longer being able to love; it means believing that we are the masters of our own *species* and that we coincide with it. If the interval between perception and recognition is indefinitely prolonged, the image becomes internalized as a fantasy and love falls into psychology.

In the Middle Ages, *species* was also called *intentio*, intention. The term names the internal tension (*intus tensio*) of each being, that which pushes it to become an image, to communicate itself. The *species* is nothing other than the tension, the love with which each being desires itself, desires to persevere in its own being. In the image, being and desire, existence and *conatus* coincide perfectly. To love another being means to desire its *species*, that is, to desire the desire with which it desires to persevere in its being. In this sense, special being is the being that is common or generic, and this is something like the image or the face of humanity.

The *species* does not subdivide the genus; it exposes it. The being that desires and is desired becomes *species*, makes itself visible, within the genus. And special being does not mean the individual, identified by this or that quality which belongs exclusively to it. On the contrary, it means a being insofar as it is whatever being [*essere qualunque*], a being such that it is — generically and indifferently — each one of its qualities, adhering to them without allowing any of them to identify it.

"Whatever being is desirable" is a tautology.

Specious first meant "beautiful" and only later came to mean "untrue, apparent." *Species* was first defined as that which makes visible and only later became the principle of classification and equivalence. "To be special [*far specie*]" can mean "to surprise and astonish" (in a negative sense) by not fitting into established rules, but the notion that individuals constitute a species and belong together in a homogeneous class tends to be reassuring.

Nothing is more instructive than this double meaning. The species is what presents and communicates itself to the gaze, what renders visible and, at the same time, what can — and must, at all costs — be fixed in a substance and in a specific difference in order to constitute an identity.

Originally, *persona* meant "mask," that is, something eminently "special." Nothing shows more clearly the meaning of the theological, psychological, and social processes with which the person is invested than the fact that the Christian theologians used this term to translate the Greek *hypostasis*, linking the mask to a substance (three persons in a single substance). The person is the containment of the *species*, anchoring it in a substance in order to identify it. Identity papers contain a photograph (or some other means of capturing the *species*).

Everywhere the special must be reduced to the personal and the personal to the substantial. The transformation of the *species* into a principle of identity and classification is the original sin of our culture, its most implacable apparatus [*dispositivo*]. Something is personalized — is referred to as an identity — at the cost of sacrificing its specialness. A being — a face, a gesture, an event — is special when, without resembling *any* other, it resembles *all* the others. Special being is delightful, because it offers itself eminently to common use, but it cannot be an object of personal property. But neither use nor enjoyment is possible with the personal; there can be only appropriation and jealousy.

The jealous confuse the special with the personal; the brutal confuse the personal with the special. The *jeune fille* is jealous of herself. The model wife brutalizes herself.

Special being communicates nothing but its own communicability. But this communicability becomes separated from itself and is constituted in an autonomous sphere. The special is transformed into spectacle. The spectacle is the separation of generic being, that is, the impossibility of love and the triumph of jealousy.

CHAPTER EIGHT

The Author as Gesture

On February 22, 1969, Michel Foucault presented the lecture "What Is an Author?" to the members and guests of the Société Française de Philosophie.[1] Three years earlier, the publication of *The Order of Things* had made him a celebrity. In the audience (which included Jean Wahl, who introduced the lecture, Maurice de Gandillac, Lucien Goldmann, and Jacques Lacan), it was easy to confuse fashionable curiosity with excitement about the topic to be discussed. Foucault began his lecture with a quote from Samuel Beckett ("What matter who's speaking, someone said what matter who's speaking")[2] as a way to formulate an indifference toward the author that would serve as the basis of an ethics of contemporary writing. What is in question in writing, Foucault suggested, is not so much the expression of a subject as the opening of a space in which the writing subject does not cease to disappear: "The trace of the writer is found only in the singularity of his absence."[3]

But in its very enunciation the Beckett quote contains a contradiction that seems ironically to evoke the secret theme of the lecture. "What matter who's speaking, someone said what matter who's speaking." There is thus *someone* who, while remaining anonymous and faceless, proffered this statement, someone without whom the thesis denying the importance of the one who speaks could not have been formulated. The same gesture that deprives the identity of the author of all relevance nevertheless affirms his irreducible necessity.

At this point, Foucault goes on to clarify the meaning of his operation. It is based on the distinction between two notions that are often confused: the author as a real individual who remains rigorously out of the picture, and the author-function, on which Foucault focuses his analysis. The name of an author is not simply a proper name like any other, neither at the level of description nor at the level of designation. If I learn, for example, that Pierre Dupont does not have blue eyes, or that he was not born in Paris, or that he is not a doctor as I believed, for one reason or another, the proper name Pierre Dupont nonetheless does not cease referring to the same person. But if I discover that Shakespeare did not write the tragedies attributed to him and that instead he wrote Francis Bacon's *Novum Organum*, then it cannot be said that the function of the name Shakespeare has not changed. The author's name does not refer simply to civil status; "it does not pass from the interior of a discourse to the real and exterior individual who produced it"; instead, it is located "at the edges of the text," whose status and regime of circulation it defines within a given society. "As a result, we could say that in a civilization like our own there is a certain number of discourses endowed with the 'author function' while others are deprived of it. . . . The author function is therefore characteristic of the mode of existence, circulation, and functioning of certain discourses within a society."[4]

Hence the various characteristics of the author-function in our time: a particular regime of appropriation sanctioned by the author's rights and, at the same time, the possibility of prosecuting and punishing the author of a text; the possibility of distinguishing and selecting discourses in literary and scientific texts, to which various modes of the same function correspond; the possibility of authenticating texts by constituting them as a canon, or, conversely, the possibility of determining their apocryphal character; the dispersal of the enunciative function simultaneously into several subjects who occupy different places; and finally, the possibility of constructing a transdiscursive function which, beyond the limits of his work, constitutes the author as a "founder of discursivity" (Marx is far more than the author of *Capital*, just as Freud is more than the author of *The Interpretation of Dreams*).[5]

Two years later, when he presented a modified version of the lecture at the State University of New York at Buffalo, Foucault proposed an even more drastic opposition between the author-individual and the author-function. "The author is not an indefinite source of significations that fill the work; the author does not precede his works. He is a certain functional principle by which, in our culture, one delimits, excludes, selects: in short, the principle by which one impedes the free circulation, the free manipulation, the free composition, decomposition, and recomposition of fiction."

In this division between the author-subject and the arrangements that actualize this subject's function in society, Foucault's strategy is marked by a profound gesture. On the one hand, he repeats several times that he has never ceased working on subjectivity, while on the other hand, the subject as a living individual is present in his research only through the objective processes of subjectivation that constitute this subject and the apparatuses that inscribe and capture it in the mechanisms of power. This is probably why hostile critics have reproached Foucault, not without a certain incoherence, for both an absolute indifference to the flesh-and-blood individual and a decidedly aestheticizing perspective with regard to subjectivity. Foucault was in any case perfectly aware of this apparent aporia. In the early 1980s, writing in the *Dictionnaire des philosophes*, he characterized his own method in the following way: "Refusing the philosophical recourse to a constituent subject does not amount to acting as if the subject did not exist, making an abstraction of it on behalf of a pure objectivity. This refusal has the aim of eliciting the processes that are peculiar to an experience in which the subject and the object 'are formed and transformed' in relation to and in terms of one another."[6] And in response to Lucien Goldmann, who, in the discussion following the lecture on the author, attributed to Foucault the intention of effacing the individual subject, he said with irony: "To define how the author function is exercised is not equivalent to saying that the author does not exist. . . . So let us hold back our tears."[7]

From this perspective, the author-function appears as a process of subjectivation through which an individual is identified and constituted as the author of a certain corpus of texts. It thus seems that every inquiry into the subject as an individual must give way to the archival record that defines the conditions and forms under which the subject can appear in the order of discourse. In this order, according to a diagnosis that Foucault continually emphasizes, "the trace of the writer is found only in the singularity of his absence; he must assume the role of the dead man in the game of writing." The author is not dead, but to position oneself as an author means occupying the place of a "dead man." An author-subject does exist, and yet he is attested to only through the traces of his absence. But in what way can an absence be singular? And what does it mean for an individual to occupy the place of a dead man, to leave his own traces in an empty place?

There is perhaps only one text in Foucault's work where this difficulty emerges explicitly and thematically and where the illegibility of the subject appears for a moment in all its splendor. I am referring to "Lives of Infamous Men," originally conceived as the preface to an anthology of archival documents, prison records, and *lettres de cachet*, in which, at the very moment when they are struck with infamy, the encounter with power pulls from darkness and silence these human existences that would otherwise not have left any traces.[8] The grimace of the atheist, sodomite sexton Jean-Antoine Touzard (interned in the Bicêtre on April 21, 1701) and the obstinate, obscure vagabondage of Mathurin Milan (interned at Charenton on August 31, 1707) shine for a brief moment in the beam of light cast upon them by power. Something in this instantaneous fulguration exceeds the subjectivation that condemns them to opprobrium and is marked out in the laconic statements of the archive — something like the luminous traces of another life and another history. To be sure, these infamous lives appear only through quotes in the discourse of power, which fixes them as responsible agents and authors of villainous acts and discourses. Still, as in those photographs from which the distant but excessively close face of a stranger stares out at us, something in this infamy demands [*esige*] its proper name, testifying to itself beyond any expression and beyond any memory.

In what way are these lives present in the brief, sinister annotations that have consigned them forever to the pitiless archive of infamy? The anonymous scribes, the insignificant functionaries who wrote these notes certainly had no intention of either knowing or representing these men: their only aim was to stamp them with infamy. And yet, at least for a moment in these pages, these lives shine blindingly with a dark light. Can it be said for that reason that these lives found expression here and that they are somehow communicated to us and given to be known, albeit in the most drastic abbreviation? On the contrary, the gesture by which they have been fixed seems to remove them forever from any possible presentation, as if they had appeared in language only on the condition of remaining absolutely unexpressed in it.

It is possible, then, that this text from 1977 contains something like the cipher of the lecture on the author: the infamous life somehow constitutes the paradigm of the presence-absence of the author in the work. If we call "gesture" what remains unexpressed in each expressive act, we can say that, exactly like infamy, the author is present in the text only as a gesture that makes expression possible precisely by establishing a central emptiness within this expression.

How should we understand the modality of this singular presence, by which a life appears to us only through what silences it and twists it into a grimace? Foucault seems to be aware of this difficulty.

> One won't see a collection of verbal portraits here, but traps, weapons, cries, gestures, attitudes, ruses, intrigues for which words were instruments. Real lives were "played out [*jouées*]"[9] in these few sentences; by this I do not mean that they were represented, but that their freedom, their misfortune, often their

66

death, in any case their fate were actually decided in them, at least in part. These discourses intersected with lives in real, concrete ways; these existences were effectively risked and lost in these words.[10]

It was therefore taken for granted that these were neither portraits nor biographies; what binds the infamous lives to the fleshless writings that record them is not a relationship of representation or refiguration, but something different and more essential: they are "played out" or "put into play" in these sentences; their freedom and their disgrace are risked and decided.

Where is Mathurin Milan? Where is Jean-Antoine Touzard? Certainly not in the laconic notes that register their presence in the archive of infamy. Nor are they outside the archive, in a biographical reality of which we know literally nothing. They stand on the threshold of the text in which they are put into play, or, rather, their absence, their eternal turning away, is marked on the outer edge of the archive, like the gesture that has both rendered it possible and exceeded and nullified its intention.

"Real lives were 'played out [*jouées*]'": in this context, this is an ambiguous expression, which Foucault emphasizes by using quotation marks. Not so much because *jouer* also has a theatrical meaning (the phrase could mean that these lives are staged, or their roles recited), but because the agent, the one who put these lives into play, remains deliberately obscure in the text. Who put these lives into play? Was it the infamous men themselves, abandoning themselves without reserve — Mathurin Milan to his vagabondage, and Jean-Antoine Touzard to his sodomite passion? Or was it rather — and this seems more likely — the conspiracy of familiars, the anonymous functionaries, the chancellors and policemen who were in charge of their internment? The infamous life does not seem to belong completely to either one or the other; it belongs neither to the juridical identity that will have to answer for it nor to the functionaries of power who will judge the infamous men in the end. The infamous life is only played; it is never possessed, never represented, never said — and that is why it is the possible but empty site of an ethics, of a form of life.

But what does it mean for a life to put itself — or to be put — into play?

In Dostoyevsky's *The Idiot*, Nastasya Filippovna enters her drawing room on a certain evening that will decide her existence.[11] She has promised Afanasy Ivanovich Totsky, the man who has dishonored her and kept her until now, that she will respond to his offer to marry the young Ganya in exchange for seventy-five thousand rubles. All her friends and acquaintances are gathered in her drawing room, including General Yepanchin, the ineffable Lebedev, and the venomous Ferdischenko. Even Prince Myshkin is there, as is Rogozhin, who at a certain point makes an entrance at the head of an unseemly clique, bearing a packet containing a hundred thousand rubles for Nastasya. From the beginning, the evening has something sick and feverish about it. The mistress of the house never stops repeating: *I have a fever, I don't feel well.*

By agreeing to play the unpleasant society game proposed by Ferdischenko, in which each player must confess his own abjection, Nastasya immediately places the entire evening under the sign of games and play. And it is out of playfulness or caprice that she makes Prince Myshkin, who is practically a stranger to her, decide her response to Totsky. From there, everything happens very quickly. She unexpectedly agrees to marry the prince, only to take it back immediately, choosing Rogozhin instead. Then, as if possessed, she grabs the packet containing the hundred thousand rubles and throws it into the fire, promising the avid Ganya that the money will be his if he has the courage to pluck it from the flames.

What guides the actions of Nastasya Filippovna? However excessive her gestures may be, they are incomparably superior to the calculations and the attitudes of the others present (with the exception of Myshkin). And yet it is impossible to discern in these gestures anything like a rational decision or a moral principle. Nor can one say that she acts in order to seek vengeance (against Totsky, for example). From beginning to end, Nastasya seems gripped by a delirium, as her friends never tire of saying ("But what are you talking about? You're having an attack"; "I don't understand her, she's lost her head").

Nastasya Filippovna has put her life into play — or perhaps she has allowed this life to be put into play by Myshkin, by Rogozhin, by Lebedev, and, at bottom, by her own caprice. That is why her behavior is inexplicable; that is why she remains perfectly inaccessible and misunderstood in all her actions. A life is ethical not when it simply submits to moral laws but when it accepts putting itself into play in its gestures, irrevocably and without reserve — even at the risk that its happiness or its disgrace will be decided once and for all.

The author marks the point at which a life is offered up and played out in the work. Offered up and played out, not expressed or fulfilled. For this reason, the author can only remain unsatisfied and unsaid in the work. He is the illegible someone who makes reading possible, the legendary emptiness from which writing and discourse issue. The author's gesture is attested to as a strange and incongruous presence in the work it has brought to life, in exactly the same way that — according to the theorists of the commedia dell'arte — the Harlequin's *lazzo* incessantly interrupts the story unfolding on the stage and continually unravels the plot. And yet, just as the *lazzo* owes its name to the fact that, like a lace, it returns each time to retie the thread that it has loosened, the author's gesture guarantees the life of the work only through the irreducible presence of an inexpressive outer edge. Like the mime in his silence and the Harlequin with his *lazzo*, the author tirelessly returns to enclose himself again within the opening he has created. And just as we seek in vain — in old books that reproduce the portrait or photograph of the author as a frontispiece — to decipher the reasons and the meaning of the work from the author's enigmatic features, so does his gesture hesitate on the threshold of the work, like an intractable exergue that ironically claims to hold its unavowable secret.

And yet this illegible gesture, this place that remains empty, is what makes reading possible. Consider the poem that begins "*Padre polvo que subes de España.*"[12] We know — or at least we have been told — that this was written one day in 1937 by a man named César Vallejo, who was born in Peru in 1892 and is now buried in the Montparnasse Cemetery in Paris, next to his wife, Georgette, who survived him by many years and is responsible, it seems, for the flawed edition of his poetry and other posthumous writings. Let us attempt to pinpoint the relationship that constitutes this poem as a work by César Vallejo (or César Vallejo as the author of this poem). Does it mean that on a certain day this particular sentiment, this incomparable thought passed for a brief moment through the mind and soul of the individual named César Vallejo? Nothing is less certain. Indeed, it is rather likely that this thought and this sentiment became real for him, and their details and nuances became inextricably his own, only after — or while — writing the poem (just as they become such for us only in the moment when we read the poem).

Does this mean that the place of thought and feeling is in the poem itself, in the signs that make up the text? How could a passion, a thought be contained in a piece of paper? By definition, feelings and thoughts require a subject to experience and think them. In order for them to become present, someone must take up the book and read. This individual will occupy the empty place in the poem left by the author; he will repeat the same inexpressive gesture the author used to testify to his absence in the work.

The place of the poem — or, rather, its taking place — is therefore neither in the text nor in the author (nor in the reader): it is in the gesture through which the author and reader put themselves into play in the text and, at the same time, are infinitely withdrawn from it. The author is only the witness or guarantor of his own absence in the work in which he is put into play, and the reader can only provide this testimony once again, making himself in turn the guarantor of the inexhaustible game in which he plays at missing himself. Just as, according to Averroës, thought is unique and separate from the individuals who use their imaginations and fantasies to join with it from time to time, so do the author and the reader enter into a relationship with the work only on the condition that they remain unexpressed in it. And yet the text has no

71

other light than the opaque one that radiates from the testimony of this absence.

But this is precisely why the author also marks the limit beyond which no interpretation can proceed. Reading must come to an end at the place where the reading of what has been poetized encounters in some way the empty place of what was lived. It is just as illegitimate to attempt to construct the personality of the author by means of the work as it is to turn his gesture into the secret cipher of reading.

Perhaps Foucault's aporia becomes less enigmatic at this point. The subject — like the author, like the life of the infamous man — is not something that can be directly attained as a substantial reality present in some place; on the contrary, it is what results from the encounter and from the hand-to-hand confrontation with the apparatuses in which it has been put — and has put itself — into play. For writing (any writing, not only the writing of the chancellors of the archive of infamy) is an apparatus too, and the history of human beings is perhaps nothing other than the hand-to-hand confrontation with the apparatuses they have produced — above all with language. And just as the author must remain unexpressed in the work while still attesting, in precisely this way, to his own irreducible presence, so must subjectivity show itself and increase its resistance at the point where its apparatuses capture it and put it into play. A subjectivity is produced where the living being, encountering language and putting itself into play in language without reserve, exhibits in a gesture the impossibility of its being reduced to this gesture. All the rest is psychology, and nowhere in psychology do we encounter anything like an ethical subject, a form of life.

Chapter Nine

In Praise of Profanation

The Roman jurists knew perfectly well what it meant to "profane." Sacred or religious were the things that in some way belonged to the gods. As such, they were removed from the free use and commerce of men; they could be neither sold nor held in lien, neither given for usufruct nor burdened by servitude. Any act that violated or transgressed this special unavailability, which reserved these things exclusively for the celestial gods (in which case they were properly called "sacred") or for the gods of the underworld (in which case they were simply called "religious"), was sacrilegious. And if "to consecrate" (*sacrare*) was the term that indicated the removal of things from the sphere of human law, "to profane" meant, conversely, to return them to the free use of men. The great jurist Trebatius thus wrote, "In the strict sense, profane is the term for something that was once sacred or religious and is returned to the use and property of men." And "pure" was the place that was no longer allotted to the gods of the dead and was now "neither sacred, nor holy, nor religious, freed from all names of this sort."[1]

The thing that is returned to the common use of men is pure, profane, free of sacred names. But use does not appear here as something natural: rather, one arrives at it only by means of profanation. There seems to be a peculiar relationship between "using" and "profaning" that we must clarify.

Religion can be defined as that which removes things, places, animals, or people from common use and transfers them to a separate sphere. Not only is there no religion without separation, but every separation also contains or preserves within itself a genuinely religious core. The apparatus that effects and regulates the separation is sacrifice: through a series of meticulous rituals, which differ in various cultures and which Henri Hubert and Marcel Mauss have patiently inventoried, sacrifice always sanctions the passage of something from the profane to the sacred, from the human sphere to the divine.[2] What is essential is the caesura that divides the two spheres, the threshold that the victim must cross, no matter in which direction. That which has been ritually separated can be returned from the rite to the profane sphere. Thus one of the simplest forms of profanation occurs through contact (*contagione*) during the same sacrifice that effects and regulates the passage of the victim from the human to the divine sphere. One part of the victim (the entrails, or *exta*: the liver, heart, gallbladder, lungs) is reserved for the gods, while the rest can be consumed by men. The participants in the rite need only touch these organs for them to become profane and edible. There is a profane contagion, a touch that disenchants and returns to use what the sacred had separated and petrified.

The term *religio* does not derive, as an insipid and incorrect etymology would have it, from *religare* (that which binds and unites the human and the divine). It comes instead from *relegere*, which indicates the stance of scrupulousness and attention that must be adopted in relations with the gods, the uneasy hesitation (the "rereading [*rileggere*]") before forms — and formulae — that must be observed in order to respect the separation between the sacred and the profane. *Religio* is not what unites men and gods but what ensures they remain distinct. It is not disbelief and indifference toward the divine, therefore, that stand in opposition to religion, but "negligence," that is, a behavior that is free and "distracted" (that is to say, released from the *religio* of norms) before things and their use, before forms of separation and their meaning. To profane means to open the possibility of a special form of negligence, which ignores separation or, rather, puts it to a particular use.

The passage from the sacred to the profane can, in fact, also come about by means of an entirely inappropriate use (or, rather, reuse) of the sacred: namely, play. It is well known that the spheres of play and the sacred are closely connected. Most of the games with which we are familiar derive from ancient sacred ceremonies, from divinatory practices and rituals that once belonged, broadly speaking, to the religious sphere. The *girotondo* was originally a marriage rite; playing with a ball reproduces the struggle of the gods for possession of the sun; games of chance derive from oracular practices; the spinning top and the chessboard were instruments of divination. In analyzing the relationship between games and rites, Emile Benveniste shows that play not only derives from the sphere of the sacred but also in some ways represents its overturning. The power of the sacred act, he writes, lies in the conjunction of the myth that tells the story and the rite that reproduces and stages it. Play breaks up this unity: as *ludus*, or physical play, it drops the myth and preserves the rite; as *iocus*, or wordplay, it effaces the rite and allows the myth to survive. "If the sacred can be defined through the consubstantial unity of myth and rite, we can say that one has play when only half of the sacred operation is completed, translating only the myth into words or only the rite into actions."[3]

This means that play frees and distracts humanity from the sphere of the sacred, without simply abolishing it. The use to which the sacred is returned is a special one that does not coincide with utilitarian consumption. In fact, the "profanation" of play does not solely concern the religious sphere. Children, who play with whatever old thing falls into their hands, make toys out of things that also belong to the spheres of economics, war, law, and other activities that we are used to thinking of as serious. All of a sudden, a car, a firearm, or a legal contract becomes a toy. What is common to these cases and the profanation of the sacred is the passage from a *religio* that is now felt to be false or oppressive to negligence as *vera religio*. This, however, does not mean neglect (no kind of attention can compare to that of a child at play) but a new dimension of use, which children and philosophers give to humanity. It is the sort of use that Benjamin must have had in mind when he wrote of Kafka's *The New Attorney* that the law that is no longer applied but only studied is the gate to justice.[4] Just as the *religio* that is played with but no longer observed opens the gate to use, so the powers [*potenze*] of economics, law, and politics, deactivated in play, can become the gateways to a new happiness.

Play as an organ of profanation is in decline everywhere. Modern man proves he no longer knows how to play precisely through the vertiginous proliferation of new and old games. Indeed, at parties, in dances, and at play, he desperately and stubbornly seeks exactly the opposite of what he could find there: the possibility of reentering the lost feast, returning to the sacred and its rites, even in the form of the inane ceremonies of the new spectacular religion or a tango lesson in a provincial dance hall. In this sense, televised game shows are part of a new liturgy; they secularize an unconsciously religious intention. To return to play its purely profane vocation is a political task.

In this sense, we must distinguish between secularization and profanation. Secularization is a form of repression. It leaves intact the forces it deals with by simply moving them from one place to another. Thus the political secularization of theological concepts (the transcendence of God as a paradigm of sovereign power) does nothing but displace the heavenly monarchy onto an earthly monarchy, leaving its power intact.

Profanation, however, neutralizes what it profanes. Once profaned, that which was unavailable and separate loses its aura and is returned to use. Both are political operations: the first guarantees the exercise of power by carrying it back to a sacred model; the second deactivates the apparatuses of power and returns to common use the spaces that power had seized.

Philologists never cease to be surprised by the double, contradictory meaning that the verb *profanare* seems to have in Latin: it means, on the one hand, to render profane and, on the other (in only a few cases) to sacrifice. It is an ambiguity that seems inherent in the vocabulary of the sacred as such: the adjective *sacer* means both "august, consecrated to the gods," and (as Freud noted) "cursed, excluded from the community." The ambiguity at issue here does not arise solely out of a misunderstanding but is, so to speak, constitutive of the profanatory operation — or, inversely, of the consecratory one. Insofar as these operations refer to a single object that must pass from the profane to the sacred and from the sacred to the profane, they must every time reckon with something like a residue of profanity in every consecrated thing and a remnant of sacredness in every profaned object.

The same is true of the term *sacer*. It indicates that which, through the solemn act of *sacratio* or *devotio* (when a commander consecrates his life to the gods of the underworld in order to ensure victory), has been given over to the gods and belongs exclusively to them. And yet, in the expression *homo sacer*, the adjective seems to indicate an individual who, having been excluded from the community, can be killed with impunity but cannot be sacrificed to the gods. What exactly has occurred here? A sacred man, one who belongs to the gods, has survived the rite that separated him from other men and continues to lead an apparently profane existence among them. Although he lives in the profane world, there inheres in his body an irreducible residue of sacredness. This removes him from normal commerce with his kind and exposes him to the possibility of violent death, which returns him to the gods to whom he truly belongs. As for his fate in the divine sphere, he cannot be sacrificed and is excluded from the cult because his life is already the property of the gods, and yet, insofar as it survives itself, so to speak, it introduces an incongruous remnant of profanity into the domain of the sacred. That is to say, in the machine of sacrifice, sacred and profane represent the two poles of a system in which a floating signifier travels from one domain to the other without ceasing to refer to the same object. This is precisely how the machine ensures the distribution of use among humans and divine beings and can eventually return what had been consecrated to the gods to men. Hence the mingling of the two operations in Roman sacrifice, in which one part of the same consecrated victim is profaned by contagion and consumed by men, while another is assigned to the gods.

From this perspective, it becomes easier to understand why, in the Christian religion, theologians, pontiffs, and emperors had to show such obsessive care and implacable seriousness in ensuring, as far as possible, the coherence and intelligibility of the notions of transubstantiation in the sacrifice of the mass and incarnation and *homousia* in the dogma of the trinity. What was at stake here was nothing less than the survival of a religious system that had involved God himself as the victim of the sacrifice and, in this way, introduced in him that separation which in paganism concerned only human things. That is to say, the idea of the simultaneous presence of two natures in a single person or victim was an effort to cope with confusion between divine and human that threatened to paralyze the sacrificial machine of Christianity. The doctrine of incarnation guaranteed that divine and human nature were both present without ambiguity in the same person, just as transubstantiation ensured that the species of bread and wine were transformed without remainder into the body of Christ. Nevertheless, in Christianity, with the entrance of God as the victim of sacrifice and with the strong presence of messianic tendencies that put the distinction between sacred and profane into crisis, the religious machine seems to reach a limit point or zone of undecidability, where the divine sphere is always in the process of collapsing into the human sphere and man always already passes over into the divine.

"Capitalism as Religion" is the title of one of Benjamin's most penetrating posthumous fragments. According to Benjamin, capitalism is not solely a secularization of the Protestant faith, as it is for Max Weber, but is itself essentially a religious phenomenon, which develops parasitically from Christianity. As the religion of modernity, it is defined by three characteristics: first, it is a cultic religion, perhaps the most extreme and absolute one that has ever existed. In it, everything has meaning only in reference to the fulfillment of a cult, not in relation to a dogma or an idea. Second, this cult is permanent; it is "the celebration of a cult *sans trêve et sans merci*."[5] Here it is not possible to distinguish between workdays and holidays; rather, there is a single, uninterrupted holiday, in which work coincides with the celebration of the cult. Third, the capitalist cult is not directed toward redemption from or atonement for guilt, but toward guilt itself. "Capitalism is probably the first instance of a cult that creates guilt, not atonement.... A monstrous sense of guilt that knows no redemption becomes the cult, not to atone for this guilt but to make it universal...and to once and for all include God in this guilt.... [God] is not dead; he has been incorporated into the destiny of man."[6]

Precisely because it strives with all its might not toward redemption but toward guilt, not toward hope but toward despair, capitalism as religion does not aim at the transformation of the world but at its destruction. And in our time its dominion is so complete that, according to Benjamin, even the three great prophets of modernity (Nietzsche, Marx, and Freud) conspire with it; they are, in some way, on the side of the religion of despair. "This passage of the planet 'Man' through the house of despair in the absolute loneliness of his path is the ethos that

Nietzsche defined. This man is the superman, the first to recognize the religion of capitalism and begin to bring it to fulfillment."[7] Freudian theory, too, belongs to the priesthood of the
capitalist cult: "What has been repressed, the idea of sin, is
capital itself, which pays interest on the hell of the unconscious."[8] And for Marx, capitalism "becomes socialism by means
of the simple and compound interest that are functions of
Schuld [guilt/debt]."[9]

Let us try to carry on Benjamin's reflections from the perspective that interests us here. We could say that capitalism, in
pushing to the extreme a tendency already present in Christianity, generalizes in every domain the structure of separation
that defines religion. Where sacrifice once marked the passage
from the profane to the sacred and from the sacred to the profane, there is now a single, multiform, ceaseless process of
separation that assails every thing, every place, every human
activity in order to divide it from itself. This process is entirely
indifferent to the caesura between sacred and profane, between
divine and human. In its extreme form, the capitalist religion
realizes the pure form of separation, to the point that there is
nothing left to separate. An absolute profanation without remainder now coincides with an equally vacuous and total con-
secration. In the commodity, separation inheres in the very
form of the object, which splits into use-value and exchange-
value and is transformed into an ungraspable fetish. The same
is true for everything that is done, produced, or experienced —
even the human body, even sexuality, even language. They are
now divided from themselves and placed in a separate sphere
that no longer defines any substantial division and where all use
becomes and remains impossible. This sphere is consumption.

If, as has been suggested, we use the term "spectacle" for the extreme phase of capitalism in which we are now living, in which everything is exhibited in its separation from itself, then spectacle and consumption are the two sides of a single impossibility of using. What cannot be used is, as such, given over to consumption or to spectacular exhibition. This means that it has become impossible to profane (or at least that it requires special procedures). If to profane means to return to common use that which has been removed to the sphere of the sacred, the capitalist religion in its extreme phase aims at creating something absolutely unprofanable.

The theological canon of consumption as the impossibility of use was established in the thirteenth century by the Roman Curia during its conflict with the Franciscan order. In their call for "highest poverty," the Franciscans asserted the possibility of a use entirely removed from the sphere of law [*diritto*], which, in order to distinguish it from usufruct and from every other right [*diritto*] to use, they called *usus facti*, de facto use (or use of fact). Against them, John XXII, an implacable adversary of the order, issued his bull *Ad Conditorem Canonum*. In things that are objects of consumption, such as food, clothing, and so on, there cannot exist, he argues, a use distinct from property, because this use coincides entirely with the act of their consumption, that is, their destruction (*abusus*). Consumption, which necessarily destroys the thing, is nothing but the impossibility or the negation of use, which presupposes that the substance of the thing remains intact (*salva rei substantia*). That is not all: a simple de facto use, distinct from property, does not exist in nature; it is in no way something that one can "have." "The act of use itself exists in nature neither before being exercised nor while being exercised nor after having been exercised. In fact, consumption, even in the act in which it is exercised, is always in the past or the future and, as such, cannot be said to exist in nature, but only in memory or anticipation. Therefore, it cannot be had but in the instant of its disappearance."[10]

In this way, with an unwitting prophecy, John XXII provided the paradigm of an impossibility of using that has reached its fulfillment many centuries later in consumer society. This obstinate denial of use, however, captures the nature of use more radically than could any definition put forth by the Franciscan order. For pure use appears, in the Pope's account, not so much as something inexistent — indeed, it exists for an instant in the act of consumption — but rather as something that one could never have, that one could never possess as property (*dominium*). That is to say, use is always a relationship with something that cannot be appropriated; it refers to things insofar as they cannot become objects of possession. But in this way use also lays bare the true nature of property, which is nothing but the device that moves the free use of men into a separate sphere, where it is converted into a right. If, today, consumers in mass society are unhappy, it is not only because they consume objects that have incorporated within themselves their own inability to be used. It is also, and above all, because they believe they are exercising their right to property on these objects, because they have become incapable of profaning them.

The impossibility of using has its emblematic place in the Museum. The museification of the world is today an accomplished fact. One by one, the spiritual potentialities that defined the people's lives — art, religion, philosophy, the idea of nature, even politics — have docilely withdrawn into the Museum. "Museum" here is not a given physical space or place but the separate dimension to which what was once — but is no longer — felt as true and decisive has moved. In this sense, the Museum can coincide with an entire city (such as Evora and Venice, which were declared World Heritage sites), a region (when it is declared a park or nature preserve), and even a group of individuals (insofar as they represent a form of life that has disappeared). But more generally, everything today can become a Museum, because this term simply designates the exhibition of an impossibility of using, of dwelling, of experiencing.

Thus, in the Museum, the analogy between capitalism and religion becomes clear. The Museum occupies exactly the space and function once reserved for the Temple as the place of sacrifice. To the faithful in the Temple — the pilgrims who would travel across the earth from temple to temple, from sanctuary to sanctuary — correspond today the tourists who restlessly travel in a world that has been abstracted into a Museum. But while the faithful and the pilgrims ultimately participated in a sacrifice that reestablished the right relationships between the divine and the human by moving the victim into the sacred sphere, the tourists celebrate on themselves a sacrificial act that consists in the anguishing experience of the destruction of all possible use. If the Christians were "pilgrims," that is, strangers on the earth, because their homeland was in heaven, the adepts of the new capitalist cult have no homeland because they dwell in the pure form of separation. Wherever they go, they find pushed to the extreme the same impossibility of dwelling that they knew in their houses and their cities, the same inability to use that they experienced in supermarkets, in malls, and on television shows. For this reason, insofar as it represents the cult and central altar of the capitalist religion, tourism is the primary industry in the world, involving more than six hundred and fifty million people each year. Nothing is so astonishing as the fact that millions of ordinary people are able to carry out on their own flesh what is perhaps the most desperate experience that one can have: the irrevocable loss of all use, the absolute impossibility of profaning.

It is, however, possible that the unprofanable, on which the capitalist religion is founded, is not truly such, and that today there are still effective forms of profanation. For this reason, we must recall that profanation does not simply restore something like a natural use that existed before being separated into the religious, economic, or juridical sphere. As the example of play clearly shows, this operation is more cunning and complex than that and is not limited to abolishing the form of separation in order to regain an uncontaminated use that lies either beyond or before it. Even in nature there are profanations. The cat who plays with a ball of yarn as if it were a mouse — just as the child plays with ancient religious symbols or objects that once belonged to the economic sphere — knowingly uses the characteristic behaviors of predatory activity (or, in the case of the child, of the religious cult or the world of work) in vain. These behaviors are not effaced, but, thanks to the substitution of the yarn for the mouse (or the toy for the sacred object), deactivated and thus opened up to a new, possible use.

But what sort of use? For the cat, what is the possible use for the ball of yarn? It consists in freeing a behavior from its genetic inscription within a given sphere (predatory activity, hunting). The freed behavior still reproduces and mimics the forms of the activity from which it has been emancipated, but, in emptying them of their sense and of any obligatory relationship to an end, it opens them and makes them available for a new use. The game with the yarn liberates the mouse from being prey and the predatory activity from being necessarily directed toward the capture and death of the mouse. And yet, this play stages the very same behaviors that define hunting. The activity that results from this thus becomes a pure means, that is, a praxis that, while firmly maintaining its nature as a means, is emancipated from its relationship to an end; it has joyously forgotten its goal and can now show itself as such, as a means without an end. The creation of a new use is possible only by deactivating an old use, rendering it inoperative.

Separation is also and above all exercised in the sphere of the body, as the repression and separation of certain physiological functions. One of these is defecation, which, in our society, is isolated and hidden by means of a series of devices and prohibitions that concern both behavior and language. What could it mean to "profane defecation"? Certainly not to regain a supposed naturalness, or simply to enjoy it as a perverse transgression (which is still better than nothing). Rather, it is a matter of archaeologically arriving at defecation as a field of polar tensions between nature and culture, private and public, singular and common. That is: to learn a new use for feces, just as babies tried to do in their way, before repression and separation intervened. The forms of this common use can only be invented collectively. As Italo Calvino once noted, feces are a human production just like any other, only there has never been a history of them.[11] This is why every individual attempt to profane them can have only a parodic value, as in the scene where the dinner party defecates around a dining table in the film by Luis Buñuel.[12]

Feces — it is clear — are here only as a symbol of what has been separated and can be returned to common use. But is a society without separation possible? The question is perhaps poorly formulated. For to profane means not simply to abolish and erase separations but to learn to put them to a new use, to play with them. The classless society is not a society that has abolished and lost all memory of class differences but a society that has learned to deactivate the apparatuses of those differences in order to make a new use possible, in order to transform them into pure means.

Nothing, however, is as fragile and precarious as the sphere of pure means. Play, in our society, also has an episodic character, after which normal life must once again continue on its course (and the cat must continue its hunt). No one knows better than children how terrible and disquieting a toy can be once the game it forms a part of is over. The instrument of liberation turns into an awkward piece of wood; the doll on which the little girl has showered her love becomes a cold, shameful wax puppet that an evil magician can capture and bewitch and use against us.

This evil magician is the high priest of the capitalist religion. If the apparatuses of the capitalist cult are so effective, it is not so much because they act on primary behaviors, but because they act on pure means, that is, on behaviors that have been separated from themselves and thus detached from any relationship to an end. In its extreme phase, capitalism is nothing but a gigantic apparatus for capturing pure means, that is, profanatory behaviors. Pure means, which represent the deactivation and rupture of all separation, are in turn separated into a special sphere. Language is one example. To be sure, power has always sought to secure control of social communication, using language as a means for diffusing its own ideology and inducing voluntary obedience. But today this instrumental function — which is still effective at the margins of the system, when situations of danger or exception arise — has ceded its place to a different procedure of control, which, in separating language into the spectacular sphere, assails it in its idling, that is, in its possible profanatory potential. More essential than the function of propaganda, which views language as an instrument directed toward an end, is the capture and neutralization of the pure means par excellence, that is, language that has emancipated itself from its communicative ends and thus makes itself available for a new use.

The apparatuses of the media aim precisely at neutralizing this profanatory power of language as pure means, at preventing language from disclosing the possibility of a new use, a new experience of the word. Already the church, after the first two centuries of hoping and waiting, conceived of its function as essentially one of neutralizing the new experience of the word that Paul, placing it at the center of the messianic announcement, had called *pistis*, faith. The same thing occurs in the system of the spectacular religion, where the pure means, suspended and exhibited in the sphere of the media, shows its own emptiness, speaks only its own nothingness, as if no new use were possible, as if no other experience of the word were possible.

This nullification of pure means is most clear in the apparatus that, more than any other, appears to have realized the capitalist dream of producing an unprofanable: pornography. Those who have some familiarity with the history of erotic photography know that in its beginnings the models put on a romantic, almost dreamy expression, as if the camera had caught them in the intimacy of their *boudoirs*. Sometimes, lazily stretched on *canapés*, they pretend to sleep or even read, as in certain nudes by Bruno Braquehais and Louis-Camille d'Olivier. Other times, it seems that the indiscreet photographer has caught them all alone, looking at themselves in the mirror (this is the scene preferred by Auguste Belloc). Quite soon, however, in step with the capitalist absolutization of the commodity and exchange-value, their expressions changed and became more brazen; the poses more complicated and animated, as if the models were intentionally exaggerating their indecency, thus showing their awareness of being exposed to the lens. But it is only in our time that this process arrives at its extreme stage. Film historians record as a disconcerting novelty the sequence in *Summer with Monika* (1952) when the protagonist, Harriet Andersson, suddenly fixes her gaze for a few seconds on the camera ("Here for the first time in the history of cinema," the director Ingmar Bergman commented, "there is established a shameless and direct contact with the spectator"). Since then, pornography has rendered this procedure banal: in the very act of executing their most intimate caresses, porn stars now look resolutely into the camera, showing that they are more interested in the spectator than in their partners.

Thus is fully realized the principle that Benjamin articulated in 1936 while writing "Eduard Fuchs: Collector and Historian." "If there is anything sexually arousing here," he writes, "it is more the idea that a naked body is being exhibited before the camera than the sight of nakedness itself."[13] One year earlier,

Benjamin had created the concept of "exhibition-value" (*Aus-stellungswert*) to characterize the transformation that the work of art undergoes in the era of its technological reproducibility. Nothing better characterizes the new condition of objects and even of the human body in the era of fulfilled capitalism. Into the Marxian opposition between use-value and exchange-value, exhibition-value introduces a third term, which cannot be reduced to the first two. It is not use-value, because what is exhibited is, as such, removed from the sphere of use; it is not exchange-value, because it in no way measures any labor power.

But it is perhaps only in the sphere of the human face that the mechanism of exhibition-value finds its proper place. It is a common experience that the face of a woman who feels she is being looked at becomes inexpressive. That is, the awareness of being exposed to the gaze creates a vacuum in consciousness and powerfully disrupts the expressive processes that usually animate the face. It is this brazen-faced indifference that fashion models, porn stars, and others whose profession it is to show themselves must learn to acquire: they show nothing but the showing itself (that is, one's own absolute mediality). In this way, the face is loaded until it bursts with exhibition-value. Yet, precisely through this nullification of expressivity, eroticism penetrates where it could have no place: the human face, which does not know nudity, for it is always already bare. Shown as a pure means beyond any concrete expressivity, it becomes available for a new use, a new form of erotic communication.

One porn star, who passes off her efforts as artistic performances, has recently pushed this procedure to the extreme. She has herself photographed in the act of performing or submitting to the most obscene acts, but always so that her face is fully visible in the foreground. But instead of simulating pleasure, as dictated by the conventions of the genre, she affects and displays — like fashion models — the most absolute indifference, the most stoic ataraxy. To whom is Chloë des Lysses indifferent? To her partner, certainly. But also to the spectators, who are surprised to find that the star, although she is aware of being exposed to the gaze, hasn't even the slightest complicity with them. Her impassive face breaks every connection between lived experience and the expressive sphere; it no longer expresses anything but shows itself as a place without a hint of expression, as a pure means.

It is this profanatory potential that the apparatus of pornography seeks to neutralize. What it captures is the human capacity to let erotic behaviors idle, to profane them, by detaching them from their immediate ends. But while these behaviors thus open themselves to a different possible use, which concerns not so much the pleasure of the partner as a new collective use of sexuality, pornography intervenes at this point to block and divert the profanatory intention. The solitary and desperate consumption of the pornographic image thus replaces the promise of a new use.

All apparatuses of power are always double: they arise, on the one hand, from an individual subjectivizing behavior and, on the other, from its capture in a separate sphere. There is often nothing reprehensible about the individual behavior in itself, and it can, indeed, express a liberatory intent; it is reprehensible only if the behavior — when it has not been constrained by circumstances or by force — lets itself be captured in the apparatus. Neither the brazen-faced gesture of the porn star nor the impassive face of the fashion model is, as such, to be blamed. Instead, what is disgraceful — both politically and morally — are the apparatus of pornography and the apparatus of the fashion show, which have diverted them from their possible use.

The unprofanable of pornography — everything that is unprofanable — is founded on the arrest and diversion of an authentically profanatory intention. For this reason, we must always wrest from the apparatuses — from all apparatuses — the possibility of use that they have captured. The profanation of the unprofanable is the political task of the coming generation.

CHAPTER TEN

The Six Most Beautiful Minutes in

the History of Cinema

Sancho Panza enters a cinema in a provincial city. He is looking for Don Quixote and finds him sitting off to the side, staring at the screen. The theater is almost full; the balcony — which is a sort of giant terrace — is packed with raucous children. After several unsuccessful attempts to reach Don Quixote, Sancho reluctantly sits down in one of the lower seats, next to a little girl (Dulcinea?), who offers him a lollipop. The screening has begun; it is a costume film: on the screen, knights in armor are riding along. Suddenly, a woman appears; she is in danger. Don Quixote abruptly rises, unsheaths his sword, rushes toward the screen, and, with several lunges, begins to shred the cloth. The woman and the knights are still visible on the screen, but the black slash opened by Don Quixote's sword grows ever larger, implacably devouring the images. In the end, nothing is left of the screen, and only the wooden structure supporting it remains visible. The outraged audience leaves the theater, but the children on the balcony continue their fanatical cheers for Don Quixote. Only the little girl down on the floor stares at him in disapproval.

What are we to do with our imaginations? Love them and believe in them to the point of having to destroy and falsify them (this is perhaps the meaning of Orson Welles's films). But when, in the end, they reveal themselves to be empty and unfulfilled, when they show the nullity of which they are made, only then can we pay the price for their truth and understand that Dulcinea — whom we have saved — cannot love us.

Notes

CHAPTER ONE: GENIUS

1. Literally: Hence in respect to the god we touch our forehead.

2. See Friedrich Hölderlin, "Dichterberuf" (The Poet's Vocation), *Sämtliche Werke*, ed. Friedrich Beissner (Frankfurt: Insel, 1961), p. 262.

3. See Giorgio Agamben, *The Open: Man and Animal*, trans. Kevin Attell (Stanford, CA: Stanford University Press, 2004), ch. 18, which referes to Benjamin's notion of "the saved night [*die gerettete Nacht*]."

CHAPTER TWO: MAGIC AND HAPPINESS

1. See Walter Benjamin, "Fritz Fränkel: Protocol of the Mescaline Experiment of May 22, 1934," *On Hashish*, ed. Howard Eiland (Cambridge, MA: Belknap Press, 2006), p. 87.

2. Wolfgang Amadeus Mozart to Joseph Bullinger, Aug. 17, 1778, *The Letters of Mozart and His Family*, ed. Emily Anderson, 2nd ed., ed. A. Hyatt King and Monica Carolan (London: Macmillan, 1966), vol. 2, p. 594.

3. Immanuel Kant, *The Metaphysics of Morals*, trans. Mary Gregor (Cambridge: Cambridge University Press, 1991), pp. 269–70.

4. Quoted in Walter Benjamin, "Franz Kafka," *Selected Writings, Volume 2, 1927–1934*, ed. Michael W. Jennings, Howard Eiland, and Gary Smith, trans. Rodney Livingstone (Cambridge, MA: Harvard University Press, 1999), p. 798.

5. Franz Kafka, Diary entry for October 18, 1921, *The Diaries of Franz Kafka, 1910–1923*, ed. Max Brod (New York: Schocken, 1948–49), p. 393.

CHAPTER THREE: JUDGMENT DAY

1. Walter Benjamin, "Julien Green," *Selected Writings, Volume 2, 1927–1934*, ed. Michael W. Jennings, Howard Eiland, and Gary Smith, trans. Rodney Livingstone (Cambridge, MA: Harvard University Press, 1999), p. 333.

2. Walter Benjamin, "Little History of Photography," *Selected Writings, Volume 2*, p. 510.

CHAPTER FOUR: THE ASSISTANTS

1. Walter Benjamin, "Franz Kafka," *Selected Writings, Volume 2, 1927–1934*, ed. Michael W. Jennings, Howard Eiland, and Gary Smith, trans. Rodney Livingstone (Cambridge, MA: Harvard University Press, 1999), p. 799.

2. Carlo Collodi, *The Adventures of Pinocchio: Story of a Puppet*, ed. and trans. Nicolas J. Perella (Berkeley: University of California Press, 1986), p. 89.

3. *Ibid.*, p. 347.

4. Ibn al-'Arabi, *The Meccan Revelations*, ed. Michel Chodkiewicz (Paris: Sindbard, 1989), pp. 119–47.

5. *Ibid.*, p. 120.

6. Walter Benjamin, "Berlin Childhood around 1900," *Selected Writings, Volume 3, 1935–1938*, ed. Howard Eiland and Michael W. Jennings, trans. Edmond Jephcott (Cambridge, MA: Harvard University Press, 2002), pp. 384–85.

CHAPTER FIVE: PARODY

1. Elsa Morante, *L'isola di Arturo* (Turin: Einaudi, 1957), p. 316, translated as *Arturo's Island* by Isabel Quigly (New York: Knopf, 1959), p. 308 (this translation gives *Parodia* as "Grotesque" in this passage).

2. Morante, *L'isola di Arturo*, p. 317; *Arturo's Island*, p. 309 (translation emended).

3. Morante, *L'isola di Arturo*, p. 339; *Arturo's Island*, p. 332 (here the translation also uses "Grotesque").

4. Aristotle, *Poetics* ch. 2.

5. Cicero, *Orator ad M. Brutum* 17. 54.

6. Edmondo de Amicis, *Heart: A School-Boy's Journal* (1886; New York: Crowell, 1901).

7. Friedrich Nietzsche to Jacob Burkhardt, Jan. 6, 1889, *The Portable Nietzsche*, ed. Walter Kaufmann (New York: Viking, 1954), pp. 685 and 687.

8. Audigier, in Paul Brians (ed.), *Bawdy Tales from the Courts of Medieval France* (New York: Harper and Row, 1972), pp. 57 and 66. Translation emended in accordance with Agamben's Italian version.

9. Morante, *L'isola di Arturo*, p. 7; *Arturo's Island*, p. v (translation emended).

10. See, for example, Guglielmo Gorni, "Parodia e scrittura in Dante," in Giovanni Barblan (ed.), *Dante e la Bibbia* (Florence: Olschki, 1988), pp. 323–40.

11. See Elsa Morante, *History: A Novel*, trans. William Weaver (New York: Knopf, 1977), and Pier Paolo Pasolini, *Salò, or The 120 Days of Sodom* (1975).

12. Elsa Morante, "Alla favola," *Alibi* (Turin: Einaudi, 2004).

13. Morante, *L'isola di Arturo*, p. 379; *Arturo's Island*, p. 372 (translation emended).

CHAPTER EIGHT: THE AUTHOR AS GESTURE

1. Michel Foucault, "What Is an Author?" in *Aesthetics, Method and Epistemology*, ed. James D. Faubion, trans. Robert Hurley (New York: New Press, 1998), pp. 205–22.

2. Samuel Beckett, "Texts for Nothing," *The Complete Short Prose, 1929–1989*, ed. S.E. Gontarski (New York: Grove Press, 1995), p. 109.

3. Foucault, "What Is an Author?" p. 207.

4. *Ibid.*, p. 211 (translation emended).

5. *Ibid.*, p. 217.

6. Michel Foucault, "Foucault," *Aesthetics, Method and Epistemology*, p. 462. This is an encyclopedia article that Foucault wrote in the third person about himself — TRANS.

7. Michel Foucault, *Dits et écrits, 1954–1988, Volume 1* (Paris: Gallimard, 1994), p. 817.

8. Michel Foucault, "Lives of Infamous Men," *Power*, ed. James D. Faubion, trans. Robert Hurley (New York: New Press, 2000).

9. The ambiguity of this French word (interpolated both by Agamben and by Foucault's English translator) is explained below — TRANS.

10. Foucault, "Lives of Infamous Men," p. 160 (translation emended).

11. Fyodor Dostoevsky, *The Idiot*, trans. Alan Myers (Oxford: Oxford University Press, 1992), pp. 143–86.

12. "Father dust who rises from Spain." César Vallejo, *The Complete Posthumous Poetry*, trans. Clayton Eshleman and José Rubia Barcia (Berkeley: University of California Press, 1978), p. 262.

CHAPTER NINE: IN PRAISE OF PROFANATION

1. Justinian, *Digesta* 11.7.2.

2. Henri Hubert and Marcel Mauss, *Sacrifice: Its Nature and Function*, trans. W.D. Halls (Chicago: University of Chicago Press, 1964).

3. Emile Benveniste, "Le jeu comme structure," *Deucalion* 2 (1947), p. 165.

4. Walter Benjamin, "Franz Kafka," *Selected Writings, Volume 2, 1927–1934*, ed. Michael W. Jennings, Howard Eiland, and Gary Smith (Cambridge, MA: Belknap Press, 1999), p. 815.

5. Walter Benjamin, "Capitalism as Religion," *Selected Writings, Volume 1, 1913–1926*, ed. Marcus Bullock and Michael W. Jennings (Cambridge, MA: Belknap Press, 1999), p. 288. Translation emended in accordance with Agamben's Italian version — TRANS.

6. *Ibid.*, pp. 288–89 (translation emended).

7. *Ibid.*, p. 289 (translation emended).

8. *Ibid.*

9. *Ibid.*, p. 289.

10. John XXII, *Ad Conditorem Canonum* (1322), in *Corpus Iuris Canonici*, ed. Emil Ludwig Richter and Emil Friedberg (Leipzig: Bernhard Tauchnitz, 1881), vol. 2, pp. 1227–28.

11. Italo Calvino, "I linguaggi del sogno" Conference, Fondazione Cini, Venice, Aug. 20–Sept. 18, 1982.

12. Luis Buñuel, *Le fantôme de la liberté* (1974).

13. Walter Benjamin, "Eduard Fuchs: Collector and Historian," *Selected Writings, Volume 3, 1935–1938*, ed. Howard Eiland and Michael W. Jennings, trans. Edmond Jephcott (Cambridge, MA: Belknap Press, 2002), p. 300, n. 71.

Zone Books series design by Bruce Mau
Typesetting by Archetype